Secret Church
Your Invitation To The Coming Underground Church

by Maurice Smith

**© 2016 Copyright Rising River Media
All Rights Reserved**

© 2016 Copyright Rising River Media.
All rights reserved.

Written permission must be secured from the publisher to use or reproduce any part of this work in any form except where quotations are accompanied by a full and accurate recitation of the work's full title, the publisher, and the publisher's address. Additional copies of this publication are available from the addresses given below.

Published by:

Rising River Media
P.O. Box 9133
Spokane, WA 99209

www.risingrivermedia.org

Cover Design: Gale A. Smith
Cover art licensed through istock.com

Scripture quotations are from The Holy Bible, English Standard Version (ESV), Copyright 2001 by Crossway Bibles, a publishing ministry of Good News Publishers. Used by permission. All rights reserved.

ISBN 13   978-0-9960096-7-6

Other Titles Available From Rising River Media

All Dogs Go To Heaven, Don't They?
Biblical Reflections On Christian Universalism and Ultimate Reconciliation

And They Dreamt Of A Kingdom
Biblical Studies In Discipleship And The Kingdom Of God - Volume 1

Preparing For The Coming Spiritual Outpouring
Reflections On The Coming Move of God's Spirit

River Houses Rising
The Rise of Safe Houses Of Hope And Prayer

Safe Houses of Hope And Prayer
Your Practical Guide To Organic Church In Your House

The Least of These
The Role of Good Deeds In A Jesus-Shaped Spirituality

The Inextinguishable Blaze
God's Call to Holiness, Repentance, Intimacy and Spiritual Awakening

When Jesus Visits His Church
A Study In The Seven Churches of Asia (Revelation 2-3)

All titles are available on our website at
www.risingrivermedia.org
and through Amazon.com

Table Of Contents

From The Author (7)

Introduction (11)
    Are You Chasing Squirrels? (12)
    Clarity Concerning "The Big Picture" (14)

Postcards From The Edge Of The Abyss (15)
    "The Lamps Are Going Out" (15)
    Against The Fall Of Night (16)
    Eight "Light Switches" (19)
    Overwhelming Pressures (33)

Shadows Of The Coming Judgment (37)
    An Ode To The Carthaginians (37)
    The Rest Of The Story (41)
    Deja Vu All Over Again? (43)
    Who Weeps For America? (44)

A.D. 410, Judgment And A Disciplined Faith (47)
    The World That Was Rome (47)
    The Day The World Ended (51)
    A Disciplined Faith (53)

Signs, Wonders And Blood Moons (57)
    The Problem(s) With "Blood Moons" (58)
    The "Signs" Of A Genuine "Sign" (61)
    The Church That Cried "Squirrel!" (66)

Which Kingdom Do You Serve? (69)
    Coming Full Circle (69)
    Secret Church And The Kingdom Of God (72)
    Vanity Fair And The Kingdoms of This World (76)
    A Time To Reconsider (78)

Secret Church (83)
- Red Skies And Leadership (83)
- Leaders Versus Followers (86)
- Organic Church (87)
- No! It Isn't Time to Dig a "Hobbit Hole" (90)
- The Future Is Here (So, Where Are You?) (93)
- 8 Commitments You Must Make (96)
- Getting Started (123)
- Secret Church Versus Default Church (125)
- The Urgency Of The Hour (131)

Underground Church (133)
- Where Are The Lifeboats? (133)
- Who Do You Trust? (136)
- Early Christian Networks (137)
- The Underground Railroad Network (140)
- The Hiding Place Network (141)
- The Importance of Networks (142)
- Back To The Future (146)
- Deja vu All Over Again? (149)
- Characteristics of Underground Secret Church (150)
- Where To Begin (153)
- More Ideas For Building Your Secret Church Network (156)
- People To Avoid (159)
- Secret Church Leadership (161)
- Beginning Suggestions (162)

From The Author

Welcome to a book that has been twenty years in the making. Yes, it was roughly twenty years ago when God first spoke to me that an underground Church was coming. In my youthful enthusiasm I began researching underground Churches and resistance movements and did some initial writing on the subject. But for the next 20 years God's quiet and persistent word to me was, *"Yes, but not yet."* Then, recently, His word changed. He dropped the "not yet" part and simply said "Yes," giving me the permission I needed to write this book.

I want to be clear on a couple of things at the outset. **First**, like Amos, I am neither a prophet nor the son of a prophet (Amos 7:14). I don't claim to have a special revelation from God for what follows in this book. I am simply a student of the Scriptures, and of the times in which God has called me to live and serve His Kingdom. And so are you.

Second, I do not claim to be an expert on matters concerning "the end-times." Just a knowledgeable amateur; a theologian with 40 years of practice who hopes to "get it right" before Jesus returns to take us all home. But one of the benefits of having been around a while is "experience." I've been to several "end-time barbecues." I came to faith during "The Jesus Movement," one year after Hal Lindsey's **Late Great Planet Earth** hit the Church and end-time fever was running high (higher than today, I might add). I vividly remember participating in campus prayer meetings during the 1973 Yom Kippur War when Israel was attacked by Syria

Secret Church

and Egypt, and speculation was running high that "this could be it." About that time, a college buddy and I drove home for the weekend. To pass the time on the trip he suggested that we listen to a taped message on end-time events by a prominent end-time bible teacher (who will go unnamed). Even after 40 years, I still remember the conclusion of his message. *"Now beloved,"* he declared, *"I'm not setting dates, but based on everything we have seen and heard, I believe Jesus could return between 1974 and 1976!"* So much for not setting dates. That same end-times Bible teacher is still on radio and television today (as of this writing). The only things which have changed in his message are the news articles he quotes and the dates he doesn't set.

I remember the widespread predictions that Jesus would rapture His Church in 1981. Why? Simple math (that nearly EVERYONE agreed on at the time, and nearly everyone denied afterwards!): Israel was re-born in 1948. Jesus will return in the generation that witnesses Israel's re-birth. A biblical generation was 40 years. 1948 + 40 = 1988. Back off 7 years for the Great Tribulation. ERGO: The rapture will occur in 1981. Not since the Millerite controversy of the 1840s had there been such widespread speculation that the return of Jesus could be at hand. And like the Millerites in 1843, when the agreed upon time came and went with no rapture, many professing Christians lost their faith over this failed end-time prediction. I could cite more examples, and so could you! But I won't, because I think you get the point.

I want to make something absolutely clear at this point. I

Author

believe that Jesus is coming again - bodily, visibly, in clouds of glory - and I believe it will be in my lifetime (which means He needs to step things up, 'cause the clock is ticking!). I also believe that the re-establishment of National Israel in its biblical homeland represents God's "end-time mile marker." It tells us that His return - and all those cataclysmic events associated with His return - is near. But that is ALL it tells us. It offers no guide as to the timing of those events or the timing of His return. "Near" could mean 100 years or more (although I personally hope not!), which in God's timing is nothing more than the blink of an eye. And, yes, I believe there will be supernatural signs which presage His return. It won't be a "blood moon" or a "tetrad of blood moons" that any secular astronomer could predict and explain away. The signs portending Jesus return will be like the miraculous signs/judgments God sent on Egypt and which the royal magicians of Egypt could neither duplicate nor explain, finally declaring *"This is the finger of God"* (Exodus 8:18-19).

Who This Book Is For

I hope that by now I have piqued your interest and caused you to wonder if this book just might be what you've been looking for. Let me help.

If you're frustrated with chasing blood moons and prophecies that the rapture will happen on the next "Feast of Whatever," then this book is for you.

If you believe that our culture is collapsing around us, that

Secret Church

judgment is coming and that "Church" as we have known it is in serious trouble, then this book is for you.

If you have wondered what the Church is supposed to be doing - and how we're supposed to be doing it - while we expectantly await Jesus' soon return, then this book is for you.

This book is an appeal to you and all Christians to stop chasing "squirrels"[1] and to focus on what it means to be "disciples of the Kingdom" and the Church at the End of the Age. But, be warned! Prepare to have your paradigm[2] challenged and shaken and maybe even broken, to finally be replaced with one that is more appropriate for the times in which we live.

Consider this your calling to Secret Church. The rest of this book will help you get there.

---

[1] In this book, a "squirrel" is anything that grabs our attention, distracting us and taking us away from what God has called us to be and to do. Think of it this way: If it isn't the Kingdom, then it's probably a "squirrel."

[2] That's the mental structure, framework or "worldview" you use to make sense of things around you.

Introduction

The world is changed.
I feel it in the water;
I feel it in the earth;
I smell it in the air;
Much that once was is lost,
For none now live who remember it.
"The Lord of the Rings: The Fellowship of the Ring"

The world is indeed changing.
Church as you have known it is about to disappear.
Secret Church is coming.
An underground Church is coming.

If you don't already understand this, you really are late to the party. The goal of this book is to bring you up to date on what is happening, and to invite you to join in.

Our culture - and everything which is a part of that culture - is collapsing around us. The "house" that Christianity built over a period of 1,700 years is in the last stages of being systematically demolished by forces which prefer darkness rather than light. And if this comes as a surprise to you, then I can only conclude that for you, "denial" is still a river in Egypt (O.K., I'll wait for you. It'll come to you in a minute or two). The question now facing every Christian believer and "disciple of the Kingdom" is whether to stay where you are and be a participant and a victim of that collapse, or whether to choose to be part of God's next great move in Secret Church. The choice is yours. But, be warned. This choice is NOT going to go away. It will be increasingly forced upon you

Secret Church

and every genuine believer in Jesus and the Kingdom. For you and your house, it's time to choose. Others may put off the choice in the hope that perhaps I'm wrong and that better times lie ahead. But for you, it's time to choose. And as the old knight in *"Indiana Jones And The Last Crusade"* warned, "Choose well."

Everything you know is about to change. One morning, in the near future, you will wake up, turn on the morning news and discover that the world you once knew is

> *Everything you know is about to change.*

gone. It has happened before throughout history. It happened to Christians on August 24, in A.D. 410, and it will soon happen to you. It will be like 9/11 all over again . . . only worse. 9/11 was the warning. This will be the main event. But will you understand what it all means? You will, if you read this book and embrace its message.

Are You Chasing Squirrels?

Writing books to predict "the coming collapse" or "the end of the world" has become a major industry in recent years. Why? Because we all "know" something is coming. We all know things are changing, and NOT for the better! And we all know that things cannot continue going the way they are without reaching a crisis. Even for those of us who have studied "cultural apologetics" over the years, the speed at which profound changes have recently occurred is absolutely

Introduction

breath-taking. And the speed seems to be accelerating![3]

Anyone with an internet connection can quickly find enough bad news to make an impressive list of actual or pending disasters. Likewise, a more positive-minded person could just as easily make an impressive list of good people doing wonderful things. As a result, all too often Christians find themselves chasing "squirrels"; chasing after the latest internet craze; the latest "harbinger" or "shemita" or "blood moon" or "the Feast of Whatever." But God doesn't govern the universe on the basis of "he who has the longest list wins." Biblically speaking, He expects discernment among His people. The difference between the fool and the wise man is his (or her) ability to discern the times in which they live; to distinguish between chasing "squirrels" and recognizing the signs of the times; to distinguish between the kingdoms of this world and the Kingdom of God. Do you know the difference?

> *The difference between the fool and the wise man is his (or her) ability to discern the times in which they live.*

---

[3]"Cultural Apologetics" is a branch of general Christian "Apologetics" (defenses of the faith) and focuses its efforts on explaining Christianity within the context of the culture of which it is a part; in our case, the impact of historic Christian faith upon Western Civilization (primarily North America and Europe). Prominent cultural apologists would include people such as G.K.Chesteton, C.S. Lewis, Francis A. Schaeffer, Charles Colson, Oz Guiness and Ravi Zacharias.

Secret Church

Clarity Concerning "The Big Picture"

I want us to be clear from the outset concerning the thesis of this book. Clarity concerning "the big picture" will prevent us from getting lost or distracted amidst the details of the discussion. Civilization as we have known and experienced it in the West (particularly North America and Europe) is staring into an Abyss of historic, even biblical, proportions. Not since the collapse of Rome in the 5th Century has the western world faced such an upheaval and its consequences. Failure to understand this reality and to appreciate what it means to each of us personally and to the Church as a corporate body will leave you unprepared to confront what is coming. The purpose of this book is to help you better understand why this is happening and what each of us must do by way of preparation and response.

Welcome to Secret Church.

> *Not since the collapse of Rome in the 5th Century has the western world faced such an upheaval and its consequences.*

Chapter 1
Postcards From The Edge Of The Abyss

"For some time now I have been convinced that this century will see the collapse of our civilization - whether Jesus returns in that time or not. Western Civilization has taken literally centuries to build. But by the end of this century I believe it will be in a state of ruin and collapse that few can imagine." - Andrew Strom, Author and Revivalist (at www.revivalschool.com)

"The Lamps Are Going Out"

Sir Edward Grey, (1862 - 1933), was a liberal British statesman who served as British Foreign Secretary from 1905 to 1916. The outbreak of World War 1 was a devastating blow to liberal Western Europe. Commenting on the eve of war, Grey sadly observed, *"The lamps are going out all over Europe. We shall not see them lit again in our life-time."*

Grey was right, of course. But his timing was off, and I suspect that he never fully understood just how right he really was.

Whenever the kingdoms of this world march, the lights always go out.

Prophets seldom do. Whenever the kingdoms of this world march, the lights always go out. The kingdoms of this world are on the march today, both literally and spiritually. As a result we live in an age of growing darkness, a darkness which the inhabitants of this present evil age mistake for

Secret Church

light. There is none so blind as the one who mistakes darkness for light.

"Again Jesus spoke to them, saying, 'I am the light of the world. Whoever follows me will not walk in darkness, but will have the light of life.'" (John 8:12)

In the Gospel of John the word "light" appears 24 times in 16 verses, ALWAYS with reference to Jesus. The writer wants to be clear. Jesus doesn't bring light. He IS light: "the light of the world." To embrace Him is to embrace the light and the "spiritual sight" which the light provides. To reject Him is to embrace spiritual darkness. Jesus doesn't offer any middle ground. He didn't intend to. The greatest darkness a person or a civilization can experience is that spiritual and moral darkness which results from the rejection of "the light of the world." It renders you blind to things that matter. It renders you blind to the approaching Abyss.

Against The Fall Of Night

"Woe to those who call evil good and good evil, who put darkness for light and light for darkness, who put bitter for sweet and sweet for bitter!" (Isaiah 5:20)

Writing 700 years before Christ, the Prophet Isaiah understood that mistaking darkness for light is common among spiritually blind

Walking in darkness, and away from the light, is a time-honored tradition among the spiritually blind.

Post Cards From The Edge

people, who mistake evil for good, bitter for sweet, and knowledge for light. Walking in darkness, and away from the light, is a time-honored tradition among the spiritually blind. It also brings God's fierce displeasure.

In the years since World War 2, Western Civilization has consciously and intentionally walked away from Jesus, the only true light. It has collectively chosen, instead, to substitute knowledge for light.

> *Western Civilization, particularly in the United States, is presently at war; not with terrorism or radical Islam, but with "the light of the world."*

Knowledge is not the same thing as light, although blind men frequently confuse the two. Our generation hates light and prefers knowledge. Light exposes sin and the dark places of our souls, and hold us accountable while pointing the way to true righteousness. Knowledge discovers new ways to commit old sins while convincing us that "it's all good." Western Civilization, particularly in the United States, is presently at war; not with terrorism or radical Islam, but with "the light of the world"; the spiritual light proclaimed and represented by historic Christianity. Make no mistake. This is a war between "light" and profound spiritual darkness. The collective "West" is at war with the faith of its foundation. And in the words of the Psalmist, *"When the foundations are destroyed, what can the righteous do?"* (Psalm 11:3).The answer is profound, if not obvious. The righteous must prepare to deal with the consequences of the pending collapse.

Secret Church

"The oracle concerning Dumah. One is calling to me from Seir, 'Watchman, what time of the night? Watchman, what time of the night?' The watchman says: 'Morning comes, and also the night. If you will inquire, inquire; come back again.'" (Isaiah 21:11-12)

Isaiah also understood a reality that we need to understand and embrace: there are times and seasons when the approaching "morning," which should bring day and light and the ability to clearly see the approach of one's enemies, brings night instead. And it is up to the watchman to know and discern these things. Postmodern Western Civilization is convinced (and wants us to believe) that we stand at the dawn of a beautiful Post-Christian, Postmodern morning, free from the repression and shackles of that ancient and out-of-date religion known as Evangelical or Biblical Christianity. In reality, night is coming; a profound moral and spiritual darkness which hasn't been seen in the West since the fall of Rome and the on-set of the Dark Ages. But where are the watchmen who should be telling and warning us?

Western Civilization - that civilization which arose out of the collapsed ruins of the Western Roman Empire - was formed and fashioned by Christianity over a period of 1,000 years (think

> . . . the Church in the West today resembles the surrounding culture far more than the surrounding culture resembles the Church.

Post Cards From The Edge

A.D.500 - A.D.1500).[4] But for the past 300 years (particularly since the "Enlightenment" of the 1700s), Western Civilization has methodically abandoned its Christian heritage. In response, the Church - Western Christianity - has increasingly fashioned, formed and molded itself around Western Culture in the vain hope that looking more like the Canaanites will somehow endear us to them and make us more "relevant." This has been particularly true in the period since World War 2. As a result, from our corporate structures and buildings to our underlying values, the Church in the West today resembles the surrounding culture far more than the surrounding culture resembles the Church.

Eight "Light Switches"

"The days of punishment have come; the days of recompense have come; Israel shall know it. The prophet is a fool; the man of the spirit is mad, because of your great iniquity and great hatred. The prophet is the watchman of Ephraim with my God; yet a fowler's snare is on all his ways, and hatred in the house of his God." (Hosea 9:7-8)

In order to minister effectively in our culture today, we need to understand the times in which we live. We need to understand why old institutions and old ways of operating are

---

[4]Documented by Christopher Henry Dawson, ***Religion and the Rise of Western Culture***, (New York: Sheed And Ward, 1951), consisting of his Gifford Lectures at St. Andrews University. See also, Arend Theodoor Van Leeuwen, ***Christianity In World History***, (Charles Scribner's Sons: New York, 1964).

Secret Church

no longer effective. We need to understand the "cultural rot" that now pervades both the world and the Church. We can no longer assume a certain level of Judeo-Christian heritage or Christian background as a jumping-off point for our presentation of the Gospel. To make such assumptions is to live in the world of the 1930s or '40s or '50s, a world that no longer exists, except in black and white T.V. shows, where Tennessee Ernie Ford (against the advice of the network media consultants) always ended his weekly television variety show with a hymn (Ford's "hymn sing" was so successful that other variety show hosts began doing the same thing).

C. S. Lewis once observed that popular culture is like "the road into Jerusalem" (what I like to call the "suburbs of Jerusalem.") A Judeo-Christian culture that resonates with biblical values, symbols and thought processes prepares the mind

> *In the West, our Judeo-Christian "suburbs" are being quickly razed to the ground by the all-consuming fires of Post-Christian Postmodernism.*

(if not the heart) to consider the claims of the Gospel.[5] In the West, our Judeo-Christian "suburbs" are being quickly razed to the ground by the all-consuming fires of Post-Christian Postmodernism. What does that mean in practical terms? It

---

[5]See *"Christianity and Culture"* in C.S. Lewis, **Christian Reflections** (Grand Rapids: William B. Eerdmans Publishing Co., 1967, 1995), pp. 12-36.

Post Cards From The Edge

means that the 10 Commandments must be removed from public buildings, public nativity scenes must go, the Pledge of Allegiance must be attacked, the Boy Scouts must accept atheists (so much for my "God & Country Award") and gay leaders, and Christian campus ministries must sign agreements not to discriminate on the basis of "religion" when it comes to the leadership of their groups or face losing their status as "approved" campus groups (these are examples of what is known as "deconstructionist Postmodernism"). I could offer more examples, but I think you get the point.

History records that in the years leading up to the Third Punic War (ca. 201-156 B.C., against the Carthaginians, see Chapter 2) the famous Roman orator Cato ended all of his speeches to the Roman Senate, regardless of the subject, with the words, *Ceterum censeo delendam esse Carthaginem* - *"Besides, I think that Carthage must be destroyed."* So too, in our Post-Christian and Postmodern World the spirit of our age seems to end every public discourse with the words, *"Besides, I think that the Judeo-Christian suburbs must be razed."* Yes, burn the past, and all bridges which connect to it, lest some innocent passerby stop, notice and ask the question, *"What do these religious things mean? Is there more to reality beyond what I see here?"* Or in Postmodern terms, *"Take the blue pill, Neo. Go back to sleep. There is no matrix and there never was."*

In honor of Sir Edward Grey, and to help you better understand what is happening "out there" in the culture of

Secret Church

which you and I are a part, and how it affects the structure and mission of the Church, I want to offer what I call "Eight Light Switches." These represent eight critical trends or events which have significantly contributed to the lights going out in our culture. These are some of the critical forces pushing us into the Abyss of God's coming judgment. So, yes, these are important.

***Light Switch # 1: The Rise of Postmodernism*[6]** - Postmodernism is the philosophical admission that there is no God to give us any "ultimate" light. We're all on our own (and how dare you say otherwise!). We all live in a shared darkness, groping to find our way in this dark world, but we all agree to call the darkness "light." Anyone who believes in the existence of "God" (as anything other than a comforting "idea" in the dark) is - by definition - delusional (read that again, because it's important as we move forward). Such people are to be sympathetically tolerated, but only so long as they don't make a nuisance of

> *Postmodernism is the philosophical admission that there is no God to give us any "ultimate" light.*

---

[6] It is not possible in this short space to fully explain Postmodernism, its origins or its impact on the Church. See our extensive article, *"Postmodernism And 'A Pain In The Mind'"* available as a PDF on our website at risingrivermedia.org. For a good general overview of Postmodernism from an evangelical perspective see, **PostModerism: An Evangelical Engagement**, David S. Dockery, Editor, (Wheaton: Victor Books/SP Publications, Inc., 1995) as well as James Sire's excellent book **The Universe Next Door** (4th Edition), available on Amazon.com.

Post Cards From The Edge

themselves by spreading their delusion and making others feel bad about themselves in the process.[7]

Light Switch # 2: The Separation of Church and State - The idea of "separation of Church and state" originated as an opinion concerning "The Establishment Clause" (found in Article 1 of the Bill of Rights) offered by Thomas Jefferson in a letter dated January 1, 1802 and sent to a group of Baptists in Danbury, Connecticut. Jefferson expressed his satisfaction that, in his opinion, The Establishment Clause built "a wall of separation between Church & State." But since World War 2 (beginning with the 1947 Supreme Court case of *Everson v. Board of Education*) Jefferson's unofficial opinion has entered Supreme Court verbiage and has been morphed into a constitutional principle which excludes any expression of biblical faith from public life. Why? The reason is simple. If Postmodernism is true (and "everyone" agrees that it is) and there is no God, then people who believe in a non-existent God are, by definition, delusional and should not be allowed to influence public policy or institutions with their private delusions.

Someone once observed that, if India is the most religious

---

[7]Anyone who thinks I am exaggerating the situation should read Richard Dawkin's book, ***The God Delusion***, Mariner Books; Reprint edition (January 16, 2008) available on Amazon.com, or follow the interviews of "Bill Nye, The Science Guy" on YouTube. These are just two of a growing number of new, contemporary atheistic voices attacking Christians and Christianity as delusional and evil. We are the source of the world's problems.

Secret Church

> . . . if India is the most religious nation and if Sweden is the most non-religious, then America is a nation of Indians ruled by Swedes.

nation and if Sweden is the most non-religious, then America is a nation of Indians ruled by Swedes. The doctrine of the "Separation of Church And State" takes this further and guarantees that delusional religious Americans will be ruled by enlightened Postmodern Swedes who will prevent the delusion from spreading to areas that might actually matter and make a difference.

Light Switch # 3: The Elimination of Prayer In School - It is important to note that lights tend to go out in cascading fashion. The cascading effect of Light Switches 1 and 2 created Light Switch # 3. If there is no God (Light Switch #1), and if all references to God, faith and religion are to be removed from public life via "separation of Church and state" (Light Switch #2; necessary because only delusional people believe this stuff), then children should not be taught, led or allowed to pray in public buildings, especially schools. But there's more. Under this new and convenient rubric, ALL displays concerning this delusional faith - things like public nativity scenes, monuments containing the Ten Commandments, singing Christmas songs in public school concerts, must be eliminated. Remember, in Postmodernism there is always a reason behind the apparent madness. There are reasons why Christian expression must be systematically suppressed and expunged from public life,

Post Cards From The Edge

regardless of public opinion.

Light Switch # 4: Roe V Wade - Make no mistake about this. The cascading effect of the first three Light Switches we have examined produced Light Switch #4. The 1973 Supreme Court Decision of *Roe V. Wade* legalizing abortion-on-demand represented the categorical rejection of 2,000 years of Christian teaching and cultural understanding concerning the sanctity of human life, created in the image of God. Christians must understand that abortion represents an attack both upon God's existence and upon the idea that we as human beings (including unborn human beings) are unique creatures created in His image, not the unlikely end product of blind random chance and evolutionary processes. But in our Postmodern world, there is no God to create man in His image or to give his life a sacred dignity above that of any other evolution-produced animal. And because there is no God, there is no greater "moral light" than scientific "knowledge" to say that abortion is wrong. And because science cannot make such a value judgment based on "knowledge" alone, abortion is acceptable, based upon the individual's personal choice. Only delusional "religious" people could think differently.

Light Switch # 5: Gay Marriage - Welcome to the uncontrolled cascade of Post-Christian Postmodernism. If Light Switches 1 through 4 are true, then there is no God to give "moral light"; there is no such thing as a divine pattern for human sexuality or marriage; there is no "higher morality" which can deny individuals the "right" to sexual and marital

Secret Church

fulfillment in whatever fashion they desire. The 2015 Supreme Court decision legalizing gay marriage embodies a logical and necessary step in the march of Postmodernism away from the delusional notion of a God Who can tell people how to run their lives. It embodies a conscious choice to reject the "light of the world" and to embrace the moral and spiritual darkness of the Abyss.

Light Switch # 6: Christian Persecution - The Light Switch of Christian Persecution is the inevitable and unavoidable consequence of the first five previous Light Switches. Such an out-of-date religion and such a delusional group of people deserve to be persecuted and excluded from public life: politics, law, government, schools, education, business, sports and more. Their Churches should be denied access to and use of public facilities such as schools for their meetings (as is presently happening in New York City). Their Campus Christian ministries should be denied status as approved student organizations if they refuse to open leadership offices to non-believers (as has happened at several universities around the country, including Rutgers, Vanderbilt and UCDavis).[8]

> *How long would your Church or ministry survive the loss of its tax-exempt status, and if they were required to pay property taxes on their facilities?*

---

[8] See our article, *"An Open Letter To The Christian Community of Vanderbilt University"* posted on our website at www.risingrivermedia.org.

Post Cards From The Edge

Christians in either business or government should be denied the right to a religiously-informed private conscience as a basis for refusing service to potential customers, or for refusing to enforce morally objectionable laws. Finally, the tax-exempt status of Churches should be revoked for engaging in discriminatory anti-gay practices in hiring, and for refusing to perform gay weddings; all violations of "public policy" (just as Bob Jones University's tax exemption was revoked for their violation of public policy on race relations). How long would your Church or ministry survive the loss of its tax-exempt status, and if they were required to pay property taxes on their facilities? And how many pastors would be financially unable to continue in ministry if their clergy housing allowance was eliminated?

Some of these things have already occurred, while others are quickly looming on the horizon. How will your faith stand up to the pressures of persecution which may soon fall on you?

> *Do you know what to "hold fast" in the midst of persecution in order not to compromise your faith?*

One of the frequent admonitions of the Risen Christ to the seven Churches of Asia in Revelation 2-3 is to *"hold fast what you have received"* and to not compromise their faith with the surrounding culture. Do you know what to "hold fast" in the midst of persecution in order not to compromise your

Secret Church

faith? [9]

Light Switch # 7: The Collapse of Politics - The intellectual father of the Moral Majority (a political movement founded by Pastor Jerry Falwell in 1979), and a "founding father" of the religious/conservative political "right," was a man by the name of Paul Weyrich.

In February of 1999, shortly after the United States Senate failed to convict and impeach President Bill Clinton, Weyrich sent an open letter to his many constituents announcing that, in his opinion, conservatives had lost the "cultural war of attrition" which he had helped launch some twenty years earlier:

"In looking at the long history of conservative politics, from the defeat of Robert Taft in 1952, to the nomination of Barry Goldwater, to the takeover of the Republican Party in 1994, I think it is fair to say that conservatives have learned to succeed in politics. That is, we got our people elected. But that did not result in the adoption of our agenda. The reason, I think, is that politics itself has failed. And politics has failed because of the collapse of the culture. The culture we are living in becomes an ever-wider sewer. In truth, I think we are caught up in a cultural collapse of historic proportions, a

---

[9]See our book, ***When Jesus Visits His Church: Studies In The Seven Churches of Asia (Revelation 2-3)*** available via our website at risingrivermedia.org.

Post Cards From The Edge

collapse so great that <u>it simply overwhelms politics.</u>" [10]

Unfortunately, Mr. Weyrich, the "Christian right" and much of the evangelical Church discovered themselves out of touch with a generation that had drunk deeply at the tainted wells of Postmodern moral doubt and skepticism. In a Christian version of Rip van Winkle, Christians had fallen asleep in Church and awoke one day to find themselves in a Post-Christian Postmodern culture that no longer recognized the values and principles they were taught to live by. Mr. Weyrich continued, *"Let me be perfectly frank about it. If there really were a moral majority out there, Bill Clinton would have been driven out of office months ago. What Americans would have found absolutely intolerable only a few years ago, a majority now not only tolerates but celebrates."*

Mr. Weyrich's conclusion came as a bitter pill to swallow, *"I no longer believe that there is a moral majority. I believe that we probably have lost the culture war. That doesn't mean the war is not going to continue and that it isn't going to be fought on other fronts. But in terms of society in general, we have lost. This is why, even when we win in politics, our victories fail to translate into the kind of policies we believe are important."*

---

[10] The September 6, 1999 issue of **Christianity Today** magazine reprinted Mr. Weyrich's letter, along with responses by six leading evangelicals, including Ralph Reed, Cal Thomas, Jerry Falwell, Don Eberly (his response is particularly good), James Dobson and Charles Colson. These are a "must read."

Secret Church

In the light of these dangers facing the Church this Post-Christian Postmodern age, the warning of Paul Weyrich to his constituents is sobering: *"Don't be misled by politicians who say that everything is great, that we are on the verge of this wonderful new era, thanks to technology or the stock market or whatever. These are lies. We are not in the dawn of a new civilization, but the twilight of an old one. We will be lucky if we escape with any remnants of the great Judeo-Christian civilization that we have known through the ages."*

> *. . . the pervasive rot of Post-Christian Postmodernism means that politics . . . simply cannot provide a recourse or remedy to what is taking place.*

I'm afraid Mr. Weyrich was being overly optimistic. Even the "remnants" are quickly being erased. Today, many Christians continue to place their hope in political action - even political revolution - for avoiding complete cultural collapse. They remain convinced that electing the right people in the next election will turn everything around. But that's like believing that appointing a better captain could have saved the Titanic AFTER it hit the iceberg. Sorry, but the pervasive rot of Post-Christian Postmodernism means that politics (conservative, liberal or otherwise) simply cannot provide a recourse or remedy to what is taking place.

Light Switch # 8: *The Rise of Militant Islam* - O.K., a little historical perspective is in order here. Islam, founded in the 7th Century A.D. in what is today Saudi Arabia, has ALWAYS

Post Cards From The Edge

been militant, and has always grown by a combination of reproduction (you're Muslim if you were born into a Muslim family) and conquest (Jihad). Within 300 years of the death of Mohammed, Islam had conquered most of North Africa, the Middle East, a wide swath of Asia Minor (Modern Turkey) and was threatening Constantinople (Byzantium, the capital of the "Eastern Empire") - the gateway to Europe. The Crusades (think A.D. 1095 - 1221, or about 125 years of activity) represented Europe's multi-faceted response to this reality.[11] The Crusades failed to stop the march of militant Islam, and by the time of the Protestant Reformation (1500s), Islam had conquered Constantinople, much of southern Spain and had fought its way to the gates of Vienna in the heart of Europe.

There is far more history here than we can discuss, but here's the point. Islam has always been militant, and nothing has changed today as evidenced by a long string of recent events: the first bombing of the World Trade Center in February of 1993, the bombing of Kobar Towers in June of 1996, the American Embassy bombings in Kenya and Tanzania in August of 1998, the bombing of the U.S.S. Cole in October of 2000, the events of 9/11, the longest war in U.S. history (Afghanistan) and now the rise of ISIL. There are good historical reasons why allowing a fundamentalist Islamic nation such as Iran access to nuclear weapons technology is a REALLY BAD idea.

---

[11]See Thomas F. Madden, *The Concise History of the Crusades*. Third Student Edition. (Lanham, MD: Rowman & Littlefield, 2014).

Secret Church

It is also important to point out that the resurgence of Islam through out Europe and America in years since 9/11 has nothing to do with "freedom of religion." In Islam, there is no such thing as "freedom of Religion." Try proclaiming the Christian gospel openly in any Islamic country of the Middle East, such as Iran or Saudi Arabia, and you'll discover their complete lack of tolerance toward any such "religious free expression." As of this writing, Christians are being systematically persecuted and slaughtered in areas of the Middle East and Africa under the control of fundamentalist Islamic groups. The only modern democracy in the Middle East, which also tolerates openly Christian ministries, is . . . Israel! The willingness of the Postmodern West to embrace Islam, while attempting to deny its militant nature, testifies to the West's profound blindness concerning its own headlong plunge into the Abyss of spiritual darkness and judgment.[12]

The current "war" against radical Islamic terrorism, on the one hand, and attempts to embrace Islam on the other hand will have the net effect of pushing the West into the Abyss. Even if the West eventually wins the military conflict (as everyone assumes it will), the contest may simply exhaust

---

[12]Martin Luther wrote: *"The Turk is the rod of the wrath of the Lord our God. . . . If the Turk's god, the devil, is not beaten first, there is reason to fear that the Turk will not be so easy to beat . . . . Christian weapons and power must do it."* Luther continued: *"(The fight against the Turks) must begin with repentance, and we must reform our lives, or we shall fight in vain. (The Church should) drive men to repentance by showing our great and numberless sins and our ingratitude, by which we have earned God's wrath and disfavor, so that He justly gives us into the hands of the devil and the Turk."* Read more at http://www.wnd.com/2015/10/

Post Cards From The Edge

what little moral and spiritual capital is left in our increasingly post-Christian Postmodern culture. And naked Postmodern materialism and existentialism are insufficient and spiritually bankrupt worldviews with which to fight radical Islam, or upon which to build a lasting culture, even when wrapped in patriotism and sung to the tune of "God Bless America."

Overwhelming Pressures

"Overwhelming pressures are being brought to bear on people who have no absolutes, but only have the impoverished values of personal peace and prosperity. The pressures are progressively preparing modern people to accept a manipulative, authoritarian government." [13]

Welcome to the "dark side" of our post-Christian Postmodern culture. If there is no God in heaven to establish law and to provide a moral compass for human behavior, then there must eventually be a god on earth to fill those roles left vacant. The moral and spiritual anarchy of Postmodernism places the government in the god-like position of making wide-ranging moral decisions for our self-absorbed culture, without the direction of any clear moral compass. Dr. Francis A. Schaeffer stated it succinctly some 30 years ago: *"If there is no absolute (or Law of God) by which to judge the State, then the State has become absolute" (God)*. According to Dr. Schaeffer, all that remains to bring about a dramatic shift of

---

[13]Francis A Schaeffer, ***How Should We Then Live?*** (Old Tappan, NJ: Fleming H. Revell Company, 1976), Page 248.

Secret Church

power to the government is a crisis of sufficient magnitude that it threatens our peace and prosperity, and demands decisive action by a powerful and authoritarian government for its solution. Like a war on terror.[14]

The title of Dr. Schaeffer's book on the decline of Christian thought (***How Should We Then Live?***) was taken from Ezekiel 33:10, the great "watchman" passage where the Prophet Ezekiel warns of God's impending judgment if Israel does not repent of its sin. The culmination of the passage comes in verse 10 where Israel declares, *"If our transgressions and our sins be upon us, and we pine away in them, how should we then live?"* While this may sound like a lifestyle question, it is not. Rather, it is a survival question. The Israelites were wondering, if everything Ezekiel had said was true, how could they possibly survive the impending judgment of God? In the end, Israel did not survive. She did not repent. Judgment fell, the nation was taken into captivity by the Babylonians and Jerusalem was destroyed.

When Dr. Schaeffer wrote his book some 30 years ago, he

---

[14]In his book, Dr. Schaeffer offered what he saw as five great pressures which could result in a profound cultural shift, even a collapse: 1) The pressure of economic breakdown, like the collapse of the housing market and the great recession of 2008; 2) War or the serious threat of war, such as in the Middle East today; 3) The chaos of violence, as we have seen in Ferguson, Missouri and elsewhere; 4) The radical redistribution of wealth, such as proposed by 2016 Presidential Candidate Bernie Sanders; and 5) A growing shortage of food and other resources, as suggested by advocates of "global warming." The pressure of all of these at once - whether real, imagined or contrived - could bring about the final collapse of Western Civilization as we have known it.

Post Cards From The Edge

was prayerfully hopeful that the coming generation (in which we now live) might listen and *"get its feet out of the paths of death and may live."*[15] Unfortunately, the decline which Dr. Schaeffer so ably analyzed and documented has accelerated during the intervening years.

> *. . . if our sins and those of our culture overtake us, like a modern day Lot who never left Sodom, and the judgment of God falls, how shall we escape?*

And the Church has been overwhelmed by a surging tide of post-Christian Postmodern paganism. Now the Church of the 21st Century finds itself caught on the horns of a dilemma. On the one hand, if our sins and those of our culture overtake us, like a modern day Lot who never left Sodom, and the judgment of God falls, how shall we escape? On the other hand, what about the possibility of a genuine movement of the Spirit of God in revival that renews the Church and sweeps millions of new souls into the Kingdom of God. How should the Church of Jesus Christ respond to this dilemma in a manner appropriate to our times?

Welcome To "The Abyss"

Do you see it now? The "Light Switches" are being thrown and the lights are going out all across the West. In the growing spiritual darkness, the Church of the 21st Century now faces a profound choice. Do we join the Kingdoms of

---

[15]Schaeffer, ***How Should We Then Live?***, page 248.

Secret Church

this world in their headlong plunge into the Abyss, or do we set our sights on something different. Far too much of what passes for cultural engagement by the Church today appears to be

> *No person, no Church and no civilization can receive light by embracing moral and spiritual darkness.*

little more than the Church following our surrounding culture into the Abyss in a vain attempt to somehow be "relevant," or in the vain hope that we can somehow "fix" what's broken. Those who are suppose to have spiritual sight are following the lead of those who are spiritually blind and who walk in darkness, while they boast of how "bright" things look. No person, no Church and no civilization can receive light by embracing moral and spiritual darkness. Such issues as abortion, homosexuality and same-sex "marriage" represent profound spiritual darkness. Anyone embracing them will find themselves plunged headlong into the Abyss of spiritual darkness. This is true of any nation. It is true of any Church. It is true of any person. It's true of you and me.

There is a fearful price to be paid for such behavior. Just ask the Carthaginians, which is where we need to go next.

Chapter 2
Shadows Of The Coming Judgment

"For when the earth experiences Thy judgments, the inhabitants of the world learn righteousness." (Isaiah 26: 18)

"The strength or weakness of a society depends more on the level of its spiritual life than on its level of industrialization. Neither a market economy nor even general abundance constitutes the crowning achievement of human life. If a nation's spiritual energies have been exhausted, it will not be saved from collapse by the most perfect government structure or by any industrial development. A tree with a rotten core cannot stand." - Alexander Solzhenitsyn

The eight "Light Switches" we discussed in the previous chapter are pushing the Church and Western Civilization into profound spiritual darkness and toward the Abyss of God's judgment. We are not the first civilization to experience collapse and judgment. God has done this before throughout history. And that deserves a true story.

An Ode To The Carthaginians

Carthage was an ancient city-state in northeastern Africa. Founded in approximately 813 B.C., she pre-dated the Roman Republic and was the chief rival of Rome from 275 B.C. to 145 B.C. Founded by those ancient shipbuilders and traders, the Phoenicians, Carthage became a great mercantile trading power in the Mediterranean. Over the centuries she expanded her sphere of political and economic

Secret Church

influence and trading contact over Sicily, Sardinia, and Corsica. Her expanding influence and trade eventually brought Carthage into competition and conflict with the rising power of Rome.

Carthage preferred mercantilism over militarism, business and making money over fighting, or preparing to fight. The citizens of Carthage were reluctant to enter military service, so the Great Council was forced to rely upon slave conscripts and paid mercenaries. Nevertheless, Carthage was able to field substantial armies under competent generals, including the great Hannibal and his amazing elephants. The Carthaginian practice of crucifying their failed generals on the city gates undoubtedly had some small degree of influence upon their performance in battle!

In the period from 264 B.C. to 201 B.C. Carthage fought two wars against Rome, known to historians as the Punic Wars. Both wars were fought to military draws, but Carthage was forced to acknowledge the political hegemony of Rome. There was an uneasy peace between Carthage and Rome for 51 years from 201 to 150 B.C. The British economist John Maynard Keynes would write a book in the 1920s entitled *"A Carthaginian Peace"* to describe the period between World Wars 1 and 2. During those 51 years, Carthage, trusting Roman representations and intentions, returned to her trading empire and prospered. Rome, however, realized that Carthage was a rival that must eventually be eliminated. The famous Roman orator Cato ended all of his speeches to the Roman Senate (regardless of the subject) with the words,

Shadows Of The Coming Judgment

Ceterum censeo delendam esse Carthaginem — "Besides, I think that Carthage must be destroyed." [16]

The day of reckoning finally arrived. In 151 B.C. Carthage declared war against the king of Numidia for repeated attacks upon Carthaginian interests. But Numidia was a friend of Rome. Rome, in turn, declared war against Carthage. Although rich in trade and population, Carthage was without committed allies, without mercenaries, and generally unprepared for war. A Carthaginian peace delegation was quickly dispatched to Rome with full authority to negotiate peace and meet all demands. The Roman Senate promised that if Carthage would turn over 300 children from the noblest families as hostages and surrender all of her weapons and engines of war, the freedom and territorial integrity of Carthage would be guaranteed (unilateral disarmament to achieve peace - guaranteed!). Carthage was apprehensive, but she complied rather than go to war with Rome. The hostages were given over and the arsenals were emptied. Carthage had "honored the treaty" and was now defenseless.

When all demands of the Senate had been met, the Roman Consuls, acting on secret instructions from the Senate, further demanded that the population of Carthage should withdraw ten miles from the city which was then to be burned to the ground (I suppose these details were somewhere in the fine print which escaped everyone's attention, or perhaps

---

[16]See Will Durant, ***The Story of Civilization***, Volume 3, ***Caesar And Christ***, p. 105).

Secret Church

were part of a "secret protocol").

The Carthaginian ambassadors were aghast, as politicians and diplomats usually are when reality sets in. They argued in vain that to destroy a city which had yielded hostages and surrendered its weapons without striking a blow was to commit a treacherous atrocity unknown to history (and to diplomats, apparently). The Consuls responded that such were the terms set (secretly, remember?) by the Roman Senate and could not be changed. When the news reached Carthage the population went berserk. It seems we little people tend to over-react to the announcement of our sellout and imminent slavery! Groups of enraged people seized the returning ambassadors, dragged them through the streets, and stoned them to death. Others simply stood in the empty arsenals and openly wept.

But desperation gave birth to resolution. Buildings were torn down for metal and timber. Religious statues were melted down to make swords. Women shaved their heads and used their hair to make ropes. In the period of 2 months the desperate Carthaginians made 8,000 shields, 18,000 swords, 30,000 spears, 60,000 catapult projectiles, and 120 ships to defend the inner harbor.

For three brutal years Carthage withstood siege by land and sea. Finally, in late 147 B.C., the Roman legions breached the city walls. The Carthaginians, decimated by starvation, fought house by house, but were eventually forced to surrender. The 10% of the population that survived the siege

Shadows Of The Coming Judgment

was sold as slaves and the city was plundered by the legions. The Roman Senate, which had "guaranteed" the freedom and territorial integrity of Carthage now ordered that the city be razed to the ground, the soil be plowed under and sown with salt, and a formal curse be placed upon any man who should build on the site. It seems that the "cultural war" really is religious in nature. And, apparently, people have known this since the days of the ancient Romans.

The city of Carthage burned for seventeen days. There was no peace treaty. The Carthaginian state no longer existed.

The Rest Of The Story

The ancient Phoenicians who founded Carthage were famous for more than ship building and mercantilism. They were also religious Baal worshipers who practiced child sacrifice almost continuously for a period of 600 years. The Carthaginian Tophet, that sacred altar and precinct where the sacrifices occurred, is the largest such Phoenician sacrificial site ever unearthed, and is the largest cemetery of sacrificed humans ever discovered. It is estimated that between 400 B.C. and 200 B.C. (until 50 years before Rome destroyed Carthage) as many as 20,000 urns containing sacrificial victims were deposited in the "sacred precinct." The Carthaginian practice of child sacrifice was well known in the ancient world. The Greek author Kleitarchos, in the third century B.C., was paraphrased by a later writer as describing the practice:

Secret Church

"Out of reverence for Kronos (the Greek equivalent of Ba'al Hammon), the Phoenicians, and especially the Carthaginians, whenever they seek to obtain some great favor vow one of their children, burning it as a sacrifice to the deity, if they are especially eager to gain success. There stands in their midst a bronze statue of Kronos, its hands extended over a bronze brazier the flames of which engulf the child. When the flames fall upon the body, the limbs contract and the open mouth seems almost to be laughing, until the contracted (body) slips quietly into the brazier Thus it is that the grin' is known as 'sardonic laughter' since they die laughing." [17]

The Old Testament prophets condemned the practice of Baal child sacrifice which had been brought into ancient Israel as a result of interaction with their Phoenician/Canaanite neighbors:

"'The people of Judah have done evil in my sight', saith the Lord . . . 'They have built the high place of Tophet, which is in the Valley of Ben—Hinnon, to burn their sons and their daughters in fire. Such a thing I never commanded, nor had in mind.'" (Jeremiah 7:30-32; see also 2 Kings 17:16-17 and Jeremiah 32:35).

In 146 B.C. the Roman Legions of Scipio Aemilianus

---

[17]See, Lawrence E. Stager and Samuel R. Wolf, *"Child Sacrifice At Carthage: Religious Rite Or Population Control,"* **Biblical Archeological Review**, January/February 1984, p. 32-33.

Shadows Of The Coming Judgment

destroyed Carthage and put a final stop to child sacrifice at Carthage. Is it possible that the Legions of Scipio were, in fact, the instrument of the judgment of God on the abominable practices of the Carthaginians? Such a principle of God using one nation to judge another can be seen in Scripture as early as Genesis 15:13, where God tells Abraham that the people of Israel will live in bondage in Egypt for four hundred years before they leave and go to the promised land. Why the delay? The reason given is that *"the sin of the Amorites is not yet complete"* Eventually, God would use Israel's conquest of the land of Canaan as His tool of judgement against the sin of the Amorite (see Numbers Chapter 21).

Deja Vu All Over Again?

In the light of recent events, we must ask the inevitable question: Are we following in the footsteps of the Carthaginians (and the Amorites)? If God used Rome to punish and destroy the Carthaginians for their practice of child sacrifice, will He be any more patient with the United States, or with the rest of Western Civilization, for our practice of abortion (and the subsequent "business" of selling the body parts of such murdered children)? In all of the wars fought by the United States from the Revolutionary War up through and including the Desert Storm conflict, the United States lost 1,150,244 soldiers killed. But since 1973 we have killed in excess of 50,000,000 unborn children through abortion. If the blood of 20,000 slaughtered children, crying out to God from the Carthaginian sacrificial altar, was

Secret Church

sufficient to move the hand of God in judgment and punishment against the ancient Carthaginians, how might He respond to the cries of 50+ million slaughtered infants; the innocent victims of America's abortion industry?

Who Weeps For America?

The Greek historian Polybius, friend of the Consul Scipio and eyewitness to the destruction of Carthage, records that the Consul Scipio stood atop a hill overlooking Carthage and the Bay of Tunis. As Carthage burned, Scipio wept. When Polybius asked Scipio, *"Is not this a splendid sight?"* Scipio grasped Polybius' hand and said, *"A glorious moment, Polybius; but I have a dread foreboding that some day the same doom will be pronounced upon my own country."* Polybius observed that it is the sign of a great man that *"at the moment of our greatest triumph and of disaster to our enemies to reflect on our own situation and on the possible reversal of circumstances, and generally to bear in mind at the season of success the mutability of Fortune."* (Polybius, Book 38.21) In the Providence of God, historical circumstances and fortunes do indeed change as God moves and judges between men and nations. Scipio at some level understood. But do we?

> *. . . in our profound spiritual blindness we appear unable to see that God is no more pleased with us than He was with the Carthaginians.*

Shadows Of The Coming Judgment

Judgment is coming. And in our profound spiritual blindness we appear unable to see that God is no more pleased with us than He was with the Carthaginians. This means that the approaching plunge into the Abyss of

. . . the approaching plunge into the Abyss of judgment will come as a surprise to people who should have known better and should have seen it coming.

judgment will come as a surprise to people who should have known better and should have seen it coming. And as America and the West plunge headlong into the Abyss of God's judgment for our collective sins, who among men and angels will weep for us? And as this plunge into the Abyss unfolds, where will the Church be? What will God find us doing? What will he find you doing? Will He find you worshiping and serving Him as a vital participant in Secret Church?

The best way to find answers to these questions is to look at a time when God moved in circumstances not unlike our own. So, that is where we need to go next. It's time to look forward . . . by looking backward.

Secret Church

Chapter 3
A.D. 410, Judgment And A Disciplined Faith

On their journey into the Abyss, great civilizations collapse first at the margins because the center can no longer hold them together; the practical effect of something I call the two great "overs": over-reach and over-rot. When the City of Rome fell in A.D. 410, Christianity had been legal for roughly 85 years and the Empire had been "officially" Christian since A.D. 380 when Emperor Theodosius I made it the Empire's sole authorized religion. Officially, Rome and the Western Empire would last another 66 years. But in reality, it all came crashing down upon Christians, the Church and the average Roman on August 24, A.D. 410. And that requires a little bit of history.

The World That Was Rome

The Roman Empire ruled the Mediterranean world for nearly 500 years, reaching the zenith of its boundaries in the early 2nd Century under the Emperor Hadrian who ruled between A.D.117 and A.D.138. From Britain in the North to Egypt in the South, from Spain in the West to Palestine in the East, Rome ruled the known world. Rome was "civilization," and "civilization" was Rome. It was during the reign of the Roman Emperor Caesar Augustus that Jesus was born, and during the reign

On their journey into the Abyss, great civilizations collapse first at the margins because the center can no longer hold them together.

Secret Church

of Emperor Tiberius Caesar that Jesus conducted His ministry, was crucified and rose again. And it was under a succession of Emperors from Gaius Caligula (A.D. 37) to Diocletian(A.D. 305) that the early Church *"turned the world upside down"* by the proclamation of the good news of the Kingdom, often under intense persecution (which officially ended with the Edict of Milan in A.D.313) while gathering in secret underground "house Churches." An Empire of 60 million inhabitants adopted the faith of a 5% minority.

But all was not well in Rome. The twin problems of "over-reach" and "over-rot" took a growing toll on the far flung Empire. The growing demand for "bread and circuses" by the restless masses in Rome (and elsewhere throughout the Empire) drove up public spending and caused rampant inflation (debasing the currency didn't help any either!). Public morals and family life collapsed, as did birth rates among native Romans. The Emperor Augustus banished his own sister from Rome for public immorality, but to no avail. The falling Roman birthrate left gaping holes in the Roman legions and forced Rome to conscript non-Roman immigrants to fill the dwindling ranks at a time when the demand upon the military to secure the borders of the Empire was greater than ever.

> *But all was not well in Rome. The twin problems of "over-reach" and "over-rot" took a growing toll on the far flung Empire.*

The Empire also found itself besieged by waves of

A.D. 410, Judgment And A Disciplined Faith

barbarians migrating from the north (Goths from Scandinavia and Germany) and the east (Huns). In A.D. 212 the Emperor Caracalla (generally regarded as the worst Emperor of his age) attempted to stabilize the growing issue of foreign immigration and financial instability by declaring that all free men in the Roman Empire were to be given full Roman citizenship and all free women in the Empire were to be given the same rights as Roman women. By this "executive action," Caracalla attempted to elevate the legal status of "aliens" throughout the Empire and include them in greater Roman society while expanding the Roman tax base, since "aliens" did not have to pay most taxes that were required of citizens. Unfortunately, the economic benefits never materialized, and the only lasting effect was to minimize the uniqueness and value that Roman citizenship had held since the foundation of Rome (does any of this sound vaguely familiar?).

At a time of great crisis requiring great leaders, political leadership declined to an all-time low. The Roman Senate, decimated by decades of political purges and partisan bickering, became bogged down and hopelessly ineffective. Increasingly, the Roman Senate yielded its authority to govern to the Emperor. The Senate pretended to offer advice and the Emperor pretended to listen, while exercising increasing "executive authority" to rule an increasingly unruly Empire. To complicate matters, Rome suffered from a succession of incompetent Emperors.

> *At a time of great crisis requiring great leaders, political leadership declined to an all-time low.*

Secret Church

The hereditary succession of Emperors begun by Julius Caesar fell victim to incompetence, and to ambitious generals who used their Legions to gain the Throne by the point of the sword, and attempted to rule the same way.

As the margins collapsed and the core rotted, the only recourse left to the Empire (which was divided by Constantine in the 4th Century into two administrative divisions: Eastern with its capital in Constantinople, and Western with its capital first at Rome and later at Ravenna) was the military.

> *But no army can save a collapsing civilization.*

But no army can save a collapsing civilization. This reality, along with the pressures of mass migration and the collapse of Rome's borders, became a painful reality at the Battle of Adrianople (August 9, A.D. 378) when an army of Goths and other assorted rebel immigrants crushed a Roman army under Valens, the Eastern Emperor. Over-rot and over-reach met reality on the battlefield and reality won. The reality of "over-rot" had made Rome's "over-reach" indefensible.

According to 18th Century English historian Edward Gibbon, in his **Decline And Fall of The Roman Empire**, five attributes characterized Rome's "over-rot" during its decline: 1) A mounting love of show and luxury; 2) A widening gap between the very rich and the very poor; 3) An obsession with sex, 4) Freakishness in the arts, masquerading as originality; and 5) An increased desire to live off the state ("bread and circuses" - a public dole which provided free food

A.D. 410, Judgment And A Disciplined Faith

and free entertainment). These represent some of the "Light Switches" which contributed to the growing darkness, and which eventually pushed Rome into the Abyss of God's judgment. All of these attributes are increasingly present in America and the West today; we simply haven't taken the time to explore them. History is repeating itself. The only lingering question is whether or not it will repeat what came next.

The Day The World Ended

The defeat of the Roman army at Adrianople, an army consisting of troops from both the Eastern and Western Empires, under the command of the Eastern Emperor, opened the flood gates for the Gothic invasion of the Empire, particularly in the West. For the next thirty years, barbarian migration (some would say invasion) into the Empire, particularly by northern European Goths into the Western Empire and Italy, continued while incompetent Roman leaders failed to lead. Finally, in August of the year A.D. 410 the city of Rome was besieged by an army of Goths under Alaric I, King of the Visigoths. Then, on August 24, A.D. 410, a disgruntled slave opened the Salarian Gate to the ancient city, the Goths poured in, and for the first time in 800 years the great city was taken by an enemy. Alaric and his army sacked, plundered and looted the City of Rome for three days.

Rome's fall had a devastating effect upon Christians and non-believers alike. Why, they asked, should the "eternal

Secret Church

city" whose beauty and power men had built and admired through the many centuries, and which was now the center of Christendom (i.e., the "kingdom of Christ") be ravaged by the barbarians. Many Christians were deeply shaken in their faith. They had come to equate the stability of Christianity with the stability of Rome. The pagans attributed the disaster to the Christians, claiming that the ancient gods had withdrawn their ancient, thousand-year protection from Rome.

When the news of Alaric's sack of Rome reached North Africa, Carthage to be precise, followed by thousands of despairing refugees, St. Augustine, Bishop of Hippo,

> *Rome's fall had a devastating effect upon Christians and non-believers alike.*

was moved to respond. Augustine labored for 13 years to produce an explanation, which he titled **The City of God**. Augustine argued that Rome had not been punished for abandoning her traditional "gods" in favor of Christianity. No. Rome had been judged and punished for her historic and ongoing sins. **The City of God** is a tough read (yes, I've read it) because Augustine meticulously documented Rome's historic sins and the many moral contradictions of its "gods," its national myths and the lives of its great men. Augustine went on to argue that, rather than looking for and pursuing an earthly city, Christians should be pursuing the city of God, *"Mankind is divided into two sorts: such as live according to man, and such as live according to God. These we mystically call the 'two cities' or societies, the one predestined to reign*

A.D. 410, Judgment And A Disciplined Faith

eternally with God, the other condemned to perpetual torment with the Devil."

A Disciplined Faith

Today, some Christians try to vilify St. Augustine because he doesn't fit into their paradigm. Some attempt to vilify him for his opposition to "Chiliasm," the belief in a literal 1,000 year millennial reign of Christ upon the earth at the End of the Age. Those who held this belief were called "chiliasts." Today we call them "Pre-Millenarians." Others attempt to vilify Augustine for his teachings concerning "predestination" which maintains that God in His sovereignty has already chosen (or "predestined") those who will be saved.

Such criticisms are easy to make 1,500 years removed from the traumatic events which helped form them. Augustine was a Christian theologian and pastor seeking to shepherd the flock under his care through the collapse of civilization as

He explained that the Kingdoms and nations of this present evil age rise and fall, and that every civilization pays for its collective sins. No one escapes.

they knew it. In the process, he produced the first Christian systematic theology and philosophy of history. He explained that the Kingdoms and nations of this present evil age rise and fall, and that every civilization pays for its collective sins. No one escapes. Not Rome. Not America. Not us. But He also demonstrated by careful argument that the Kingdom of

Secret Church

God abides forever, and that, as "disciples of the Kingdom," Christians are seeking a city unshakeable, whose founder and builder is God. St. Augustine offered a struggling Church three things which we desperately need today:

1. Augustine offered the Church a critique and an explanation of traumatic world events, one which spoke meaningfully to the times in which he lived;

2. Augustine offered the Church a theological explanation which gave Christians a larger perspective on what God was doing in the world around them during very difficult and challenging times;

3. Augustine offered the Church a pastoral response that people could understand and embrace as they struggled to make personal sense of what they were experiencing.

What St. Augustine offered was an informed and disciplined faith which enabled the Church to weather the storm of God's judgment on the world of their day, while preparing them to weather the Abyss of the "the Dark Ages"[18] which would soon follow. Isn't that what we need today?

That is what Secret Church is all about.

---

[18] The term "Dark Ages" refers to the early medieval period of western Europe, beginning with the period from the fall of the Western Roman Empire in A.D.476 to the crowning of Charlemagne in A.D.800, and more broadly to the period between roughly A.D.500 and A.D.1000, a period marked by frequent warfare and the near disappearance of urban life.

A.D. 410, Judgment And A Disciplined Faith

If America were to collapse tomorrow as a result of God's righteous judgment, as Rome did in the 5th Century, would your faith collapse with it? To use Augustine's illustration, which "city" are you pursuing? The earthly "City of Man" or the heavenly "City of God"?

If America were to collapse tomorrow as a result of God's righteous judgment, as Rome did in the 5th Century, would your faith collapse with it?

Where does your heart reside and hold its citizenship? Among the kingdoms of this world, or in the Kingdom of God.

But before we can get to the Kingdom and Secret Church, we need to deal with the "squirrels."

Secret Church

Chapter 4
Signs, Wonders And Blood Moons

It was August of 1939, during the fading twilight between peace and war in Europe. Austria and Czechoslovakia had already fallen to the advancing Germans. But as yet, no shots had been fired. Adolph Hitler was meeting with his leadership at the Eagle's Nest in the mountains of Bavaria. During supper Hitler was handed a note which he scanned and then exclaimed with a loud voice, *"I have them! I have them!"* After supper he called his entourage together and announced that a non-aggression pact with Stalin had been reached. On the evening of August 23, 1939 propaganda minister Joseph Goebbels held a press conference to announce the political triumph to a stunned world. Later that evening, there was a spectacular display of lights in the sky. What happened next is recorded by Hitler's trusted Industrial Czar, Albert Speer.

"In the course of the night we stood on the terrace of the Berghof with Hitler and marveled at the rare natural spectacle. Northern lights of unusual intensity threw red light on the legend-haunted Untersberg across the valley, while the sky above shimmered in all the colors of the rainbow. The last act of Gotterdammerung could not have been more effectively staged. The same red light bathed our faces and our hands. The display produced a curious pensive mood among us. Abruptly turning to one of his military adjutants, Hitler said, 'Looks like a great deal of blood. This time we

Secret Church

won't bring it off without violence." [19]

Now for the question: Was the unusually intense display of Northern Lights that August night a supernatural "sign" that war was coming? Many thought so (including, apparently, Hitler himself), and the world press carried articles about the brilliant displays and what they could mean. Why is this question important? Because it makes us think, and it leads us to the topic of "Blood Moons."

The Problem(s) With "Blood Moons"

Let's begin with a little quick astronomy lesson. In astronomy, there is no such thing as a "blood moon." But every astronomy student knows that light refraction through the earth's atmosphere during a total lunar eclipse frequently gives the moon a coppery-reddish hue, especially if the moon is low on the horizon (more atmosphere for the light to pass through). That's basic Astronomy 101.

> *In astronomy, there is no such thing as a "blood moon."*

In his 2013 book ***Four Blood Moons*** Pastor John Hagee proposed a new idea. He pointed out that over the course of

---

[19] Albert Speer, *Inside The Third Reich: Memoirs By Albert Speer*, trans. Richard and Clara Winston (New York: The MacMillan Company, 1970), p. 194. Extraordinarily brilliant Aurora Borealis were also recorded on January 24 and 25, 1938, prior to the March 11 invasion of Austria.

Signs, Wonders And Blood Moons

2 years (2014 and 2015) we would witness something known as a lunar "tetrad." O.K., this is Astronomy 102. A lunar "tetrad" in Astronomy is defined as four successive total lunar eclipses, with no partial lunar eclipses in between, each of which is separated from the other by six lunar months (six full moons). Got all that?

Now, lunar "tetrads" are not particularly unusual. In fact, there will be a total of 8 "tetrads" in this Century (i.e., between 2001 and 2100). But Pastor Hagee argued that this particular "tetrad" was significant for two reasons. ***First***, it was significant in light of Old Testament prophecy concerning the end-times: *"And I will show wonders in the heavens and on the earth, blood and fire and columns of smoke. The sun shall be turned to darkness, and the moon to blood, before the great and awesome day of the LORD comes."* (Joel 2:30-31) According to Pastor Hagee, this "tetrad" would be the fulfillment of Joel's prophecy (the source of the phrase "blood moon") and that the cataclysmic events of the end-of-the-age would be at hand.

Second, this "tetrad" was uniquely important because it coincided with two important Jewish feasts/holidays: Passover and Tabernacles. The April 2014 and April 2015 total lunar eclipses would align with the feast of Passover, while the October 2014 and September 2015 total lunar eclipses would align with the feast of Tabernacles. Pastor Hagee's underlying assumption (one among many) was that

Secret Church

God still runs the world, including end-time events, according to an Old Testament festival calendar (which was a lunar calendar). By doing so he failed to take into account the profound change in the "times and seasons" brought about through the death and resurrection of Christ.

> *God no longer runs the universe according to an Old Testament festival or lunar calendar.*

The Apostle Paul dealt with this very issue in his letter to the Gentile Church in the city of Colossae when he wrote to them, *"Therefore let no one pass judgment on you in questions of food and drink, or with regard to a festival or a new moon or a Sabbath. These are a shadow of the things to come, but the substance belongs to Christ."* (Colossians 2:16-17) As Gentile (non-Jewish) believers, they were being "judged" by some for not observing the Old Testament ceremonial laws concerning "food and drink" and for not observing *"a festival or a new moon or a Sabbath."* According to Paul, such things represented *"a shadow of the things to come,"* all of which had found their "substance" or fulfillment in Christ. Bottom line? God no longer runs the universe according to an Old Testament festival or lunar calendar. Jesus IS coming again, but not according to an Old Testament feastival calendar.[20]

It is ironic that three of these four total lunar eclipses were

---

[20] This was the working assumption behind Jonathan Cahn's wildly popular book ***The Mystery of the Shemitah*** which helps explain why his predictions in that book failed as badly as John Hagee's blood moon predictions.

Signs, Wonders And Blood Moons

NOT visible – even in part – from Israel. In addition, a little further investigation would have revealed that "tetrads" which correspond to the same two Jewish feasts/holidays are not that unusual. In fact, there have been eight such "festival tetrads" over the past 2,000 years: 1) A.D. 162-163; 2) A.D. 795-796; 3) A.D. 842-843; 4) A.D. 860-861; 5) A.D. 1493-1494; 6) A.D. 1949-1950; 7) A.D. 1967-1968; 8) A.D. 2014-2015. So much for this "tetrad" being unique. It wasn't.

Basic astronomy and Bible interpretation not withstanding, the Blood Moon "tetrad" took on a life of its own and became somewhat of an international sensation. Unfortunately (or fortunately, depending on your perspective), nothing "earth shattering" happened. But this end-time non-event did leave many non-Christians laughing at a Church that can't tell the difference between a lunar eclipse and the end of the world. And it left a wide swath of Christians wondering, *"What was THAT all about?"* Whichever side of this discussion you find yourself on as you read this, allow me to offer some basic observations and some perspective to clarify what this is all about.

The "Signs" Of A Genuine "Sign"

Let's begin by noting that miraculous "signs" are well known throughout Scripture. The Bible is a miraculous book from cover to cover. It documents the "mighty deeds" of God as He reveals Himself to His people, and those acts of power and self-revelation are commonly referred to as "signs." We don't have time or room here to fully explore the topic of

Secret Church

miraculous "signs." What I would like to offer you is four basic Scriptural principles - drawn from my own years of study and reflection on this issue - for identifying and understanding what is or is not a genuine a miraculous "sign."

1. Genuine miraculous signs must be more than a natural phenomenon "writ large." Let's use the passage from Joel 2 as an example: *"And I will show wonders in the heavens and on the earth, blood and fire and columns of smoke. The sun shall be turned to darkness, and the moon to blood, before the great and awesome day of the LORD comes"* (Joel 2:30-31). Basic Bible interpretation should tell us that what Joel is describing here is more than a natural astronomy event "writ large." Why? Consider this statement: "*The sun shall be turned to darkness, and the moon to blood.*" Let's be clear. Solar and Lunar eclipses were NOT unknown in the ancient world.[21] They were generally regarded as "bad omens." But whatever is happening in the book of Joel involves BOTH the sun and the moon in something that goes far beyond back-to-back eclipses (since solar and lunar eclipses cannot occur simultaneously, but must be separated by a couple of weeks).[22] The context tells us this. In addition to *"wonders in the heavens,"* there will

---

[21] NASA even has a website devoted to listing them at http://eclipse.gsfc.nasa.gov/SEhistory/SEhistory.html

[22] A good first year Astronomy student knows that a Solar eclipse can only happen at "new moon," while a Lunar eclipse can only happen at "full moon," because the Sun and the Moon must be in conjunction as seen from Earth in an alignment Astronomers refer to as *"syzygy."*

Signs, Wonders And Blood Moons

also be wonders ("signs") *"on the earth, blood and fire and columns of smoke."* Whatever is happening in Joel's prophecy certainly involves more than a handful of lunar eclipses which can be explained by a first year Astronomy student.

We also see this principle at work in the series of miraculous signs surrounding God's deliverance of the Israelites from Egypt. Starting in Exodus Chapter 8 we see that the first three miraculous "signs" which God performed through Moses in Egypt (turning a staff into a serpent, turning the waters of the Nile to Blood, and the plague of frogs) were either natural phenomena which could be explained away or which could be reproduced by the magicians of Egypt. But that quickly changed, starting with the third plague (gnats): *"The magicians tried by their secret arts to produce gnats, but they could not. So there were gnats on man and beast. Then the magicians said to Pharaoh, 'This is the finger of God'"* (Exodus 8:18-19). Genuine miraculous signs bring people to the point of declaring, *"This is the finger of God."* The recent "blood moon" craze failed this "natural phenomenon writ large" test. Nothing occurred that could not be naturally explained (and which had not happened seven times previously since the 1st Century). There was no "finger of

> *Whatever is happening in Joel's prophecy certainly involves more than a handful of lunar eclipses which can be explained by a first year Astronomy student.*

Secret Church

God" moment.

2. Genuine miraculous signs point to God at work in a particular time or season. The New Testament uses three primary words to describe the miraculous. A "miracle" (Greek: <u>dunamis</u>) describes a work of God's power and emphasizes the powerful nature of the event. A "wonder" (Greek: <u>terata</u>) is a "miracle" which emphasizes the awe-inspiring appearance of the event. This is the "wow" factor. Finally, a "sign" (Greek: <u>semeion</u>) is a "miracle" which points to something greater than itself and emphasizes the divine purpose of the event, namely, to communicate spiritual truth. Genuine miraculous "signs" draw back the curtain which separates this present age from the age to come in order to reveal God at work and to confront men with the supernatural reality of the Kingdom of God. God's signs always point to God's Kingdom work in our midst. It was true of the miraculous signs which Jesus performed throughout His earthly ministry. It will be true of those miraculous signs which precede His return. The recent "blood moon" craze failed this "point" test by failing to point to God's Kingdom work in our midst.

3. Genuine miraculous signs are intended to produce repentance and faith. God's miraculous signs are not meant to entertain us or to frighten us or to satisfy our curiosity. They are meant to challenge us and to bring us to a point of repentance and faith. For example, it was because of His miraculous "sign" at the Wedding at Cana that Jesus' disciples first believed in Him. But Jesus condemned the

Signs, Wonders And Blood Moons

residents of towns such as Bethsaida (where Jesus fed the 5,000) for their failure to repent and believe the "signs" which He did in their midst, *"Woe to you, Chorazin! Woe to you, Bethsaida! For if the miracles had occurred in Tyre and Sidon which occurred in you, they would have repented long ago in sackcloth and ashes"* (Matthew 11:21). We could sum it up this way: *Miracles* are *Signs* which cause men to *Wonder* and which point to God at work, and are intended to result in *Repentance* and *Faith*. When supposed "signs" produce ridicule rather than repentance, and unbelief rather than faith, we have a "right-of-discernment" to dismiss them as not being genuine. The recent "blood moon" craze failed the "repentance and faith" test. There was no repentance or faith, only sensationalism, ridicule and unbelief.

> *When supposed "signs" produce ridicule rather than repentance, and unbelief rather than faith, we have a "right-of-discernment" to dismiss them as not being genuine.*

4. Genuine miraculous signs must be spiritually discerned by believers who see past the "sign" to see and embrace Jesus. The writer of John's gospel that tells us that *"Jesus did many other signs in the presence of the disciples, which are not written in this book; but these are written so that you may believe that Jesus is the Christ, the Son of God, and that by believing you may have life in his name"* (John 20:30-31). And yet it is a spiritual reality and conundrum that the miraculous signs of the Kingdom and of

Secret Church

God's Kingdom work in our midst are missed by the masses who are spiritually blind to what God is doing. There is no better example of this than John, Chapter 6. There Jesus performs a miraculous sign by feeding over 5,000 people with only five loaves and two fish. But the people who witness and experience the miracle (i.e., they experienced that "finger of God" moment) are blind to the reality of what the sign means (that Jesus is the promised Messiah). Lacking spiritual discernment, unbelieving eyes looked at the sign and saw only an endless supply of bread. Salvation came only to those who looked past the sign and the bread and embraced Jesus, the Messiah.

When the signs of the end-times prophesied by Joel (and by Jesus Himself in Matthew 24) unfold, it will be clear to everyone who sees them that they cannot be explained away by natural causes. It will be a "finger of God" moment. But even then, their spiritual blindness will prevent them from understanding, repenting and believing (as illustrated by Pharaoh and his advisers). They will stare at the signs, but their undiscerning hearts will fail to see Jesus. The recent "blood moon" craze failed the "discernment" test. There was nothing there to see or discern. Just a "tetrad" of full moons which had happened seven times before in the years since the 1st Century, and which could be explained away by any graduate student in Astronomy.

The Church That Cried "Squirrel!"

One of the challenges facing the Church today is that we are

Signs, Wonders And Blood Moons

increasingly becoming "the Church that cried 'squirrel.'" Some prophecy teacher preaches a sermon that goes "viral," writes a book, or posts a YouTube video announcing the latest festival date for the rapture, the latest candidate for the end-time Anti-Christ, the next festival for the "shemitah" or "blood moon" or . . . you get the picture. Suddenly, Christians around the world respond like the dogs in the 2009 animated Pixar movie *"Up."* Someone shouts "squirrel!" and off runs the whole pack, chasing another non-existent squirrel, only to eventually realize they've been fooled again and distracted from what they were supposed to be doing.

Too many professing Christians today are living distracted lives. They have been distracted from the genuine work of the Kingdom by a constant barrage of political "squirrels," economic "squirrels," geo-political "squirrels," conspiracy "squirrels" and more. Make no mistake. As our civilization collapses around us and plunges headlong into the Abyss, and as the Church is blamed for resisting "progress," there will be more and more "squirrels" to chase and distract us from what God has called us to be and to do.

> *One of the challenges facing the Church today is that we are increasingly becoming "the Church that cried 'squirrel.'"*

What "squirrels" are you chasing? And how far are they taking you away from Jesus and the Kingdom? How are you allowing yourself to be distracted from the work of the

Secret Church

Kingdom and the mission of the Church you have been called to?

Never before in the history of the Church, since the fall of Rome, has there been a greater need for a focused and disciplined faith . . . and for Secret Church. Secret Church is for those Christians and disciples of the Kingdom who are tired of chasing the latest "squirrel" and who want to know what it truly means to be the Church and to be "disciples of the Kingdom" at the end of the Age.

Are you ready? Let's get started. And we'll begin with the Kingdom.

Chapter 5
Which Kingdom Do You Serve?

"All your works shall give thanks to you, O LORD, and all your saints shall bless you! They shall speak of the glory of your kingdom and tell of your power, to make known to the children of man your mighty deeds, and the glorious splendor of your kingdom. Your kingdom is an everlasting kingdom, and your dominion endures throughout all generations." (Psalm 145:10-13)

Coming Full Circle

We have now come full circle, back to the very question St. Augustine posed to the Church under his care 1,600 years ago as Western Civilization collapsed around them. Which "city" - which Kingdom - do you serve? The Kingdoms of this present evil age (Galatians 1:4) or the Kingdom of God? That's an important question each of us must answer. But just as important - if not more so, because of its relevance today - we have come full circle to the question the disciples posed to Jesus just before His ascension:

"So when they had come together, they asked him, 'Lord, will you at this time restore the kingdom to Israel?' He said to them, 'It is not for you to know times or seasons that the Father has fixed by his own authority. But you will receive power when the Holy Spirit has come upon you, and you will be my witnesses in Jerusalem and in all Judea and Samaria, and to the end of the earth.'" (Acts 1:6-8)

Secret Church

Why is this important now? Because this represents their 1st Century "rapture" question. For the disciples to ask Jesus if it was time to *"restore the Kingdom to Israel"* (i.e., set up His earthly Millennial Kingdom) is like the Church today asking,

> *And if Jesus were here today, I believe He would give us the same answer He gave His disciples 2,000 years ago.*

"Lord, is it time now for the rapture?" Isn't this the question many Bible-believing Christians are asking today? Isn't this the real question behind all of the "blood moon" and "harbinger" and "shemitah" controversies? Of course it is! And if Jesus were here today, I believe He would give us the same answer He gave His disciples 2,000 years ago.

Jesus' answer is structured as a strong prohibition, followed by a two-fold promise, and is much clearer and stronger in the Greek than in most English translations: **"NOT** this . . . **BUT** this." [23] It's as if Jesus was emphasizing to His disciples (and us!), *"No, don't focus on that, because it's none of your business; but focus instead on the power I am going to give you to be my witnesses to the nations!"* According to Jesus' words here, each of us has a choice to make. We must

---

[23] The first clause (*"It is not for you to know"*) begins with a strong Greek negation (ουκ), while the second clause (*"but you will receive power. . ."*) begins with a strong disjunctive (αλλα). In ***A Manual Grammar of the Greek Testament***, Dana and Mantey state that ουχ *"denies the reality of an alleged fact. It is the clear-cut, point-blank negative, objective, final"* (Page 264). Likewise, αλλα, *"is a strong adversative conjunction"* with *"emphatic force"* (Page 240).

Which Kingdom Do You Serve?

choose between greater knowledge of end-time events (knowledge which Jesus says is NOT available to us) on the one hand, or power to be His witnesses to the nations on the other hand. You would think this would be a clear and easy choice, a "no-brainer." And, yet, Christians seem to continually make the wrong choice, urged on by end-time prophecy teachers claiming to have knowledge of things Jesus said we couldn't know. What will your choice be? Because, it's time to choose. Which kingdom do you serve? And do you want knowledge you can't have, or do you want power to be His witness?

Is Jesus coming again? Yes, He is! And as the early Christians declared, "Maranatha!" Our Lord, Come! Could His return be soon? Yes, it could. Or it could be 100 years from now (which is barely a "blink of the eye" on God's timetable). Jesus' point to

The Church that is focused on taking the good news of Jesus and the Kingdom to the ends of the earth . . . is the Church which is truly ready to greet Jesus upon His return.

His disciples - and to us - is that we need to get our focus off trying to predict His return and focus our attention on what it means to be His witnesses to the nations. The Church that is focused on taking the good news of Jesus and the Kingdom to the ends of the earth - even in the midst of great upheaval and the rise and fall of nations - is the Church which is truly ready to greet Jesus upon His return, whether His coming is tomorrow, next year or 100 years from now.

Secret Church

Are you ready?

Secret Church And The Kingdom Of God

"And in the days of those kings the God of heaven will set up a kingdom that shall never be destroyed, nor shall the kingdom be left to another people. It shall break in pieces all these kingdoms and bring them to an end, and it shall stand forever." (Daniel 2:44)

We opened this chapter with a passage of Scripture from Psalm 145. No passage anywhere in Scripture speaks more eloquently about the Kingdom of God than this passage by the Old Testament Psalmist. In language both poetically beautiful and theologically profound - penned nearly a thousand years before Jesus - the Psalmist demonstrates that the people of God have always known and understood something about the Kingdom of God. In the process the Psalmist defines the Kingdom of God: it is Jehovah's kingly rule, what the Psalmist refers to as His "dominion." Both the Psalmist and the people of God understood that the Kingdom of God means that Jehovah reigns as "King" and that His reign knows no boundaries of space, time or geography.

This passage from the Psalmist, along with the above passage from the book of Daniel, tells us that the Kingdom has always been God's "big picture." Everything God has done throughout

> *. . . the Kingdom has always been God's "big picture."*

Which Kingdom Do You Serve?

Scripture, everything He is doing in the world today, and everything He will do from now until Jesus returns, is about re-establishing His Kingly rule over the hearts and lives of His rebellious creatures. And to re-establish His Kingly rule, God now calls all men everywhere to repent of their sin and rebellion and to believe in His Messiah-King, Jesus. Through Jesus, God is redeeming His rebellious creatures, delivering them from the domain of darkness which rules this present evil age and bringing them into the Kingdom of His beloved Son (Colossians 1:13-14).

Welcome to the Kingdom of God and to Secret Church. Secret Church begins with each of us coming to a fresh understanding of the heart and purpose of God for His Kingdom, and then re-orienting the focus of our lives and ministries away from the kingdoms of this world and toward the reality of the Kingdom of God and what it means for us to be disciples of that Kingdom. The New Testament has much to say about the Kingdom of God. I want to touch on two major points, and then pray that your own spiritual hunger and integrity will motivate you to explore more.[24]

---

[24] I have written much more concerning the Kingdom of God, its relationship to the Church and what it means for us to be "disciples of the Kingdom," material which we simply don't have the time and space to repeat here. I would encourage the reader to read Chapters 1 through 6 of my book, ***And They Dreamt Of A Kingdom: Biblical Studies In Discipleship And The Kingdom of God - Volume 1***, available thru our website at risingrivermedia.org. I would also highly recommend George Eldon Ladd, ***The Gospel Of The Kingdom: Scriptural Studies In The Kingdom of God*** (Grand Rapids: William B. Eerdmans Publishing Company, 1959, 1990).

Secret Church

First, Jesus was all about the Kingdom. *"From that time Jesus began to preach, saying, 'Repent, for the kingdom of heaven is at hand.'"* (Matthew 4:17) In three years of ministry as recorded in four Gospels,

> *If our message or ministry can be understood apart from the Kingdom of God, it isn't the message or ministry of Jesus.*

Jesus either referred to or taught about the Kingdom of God over 100 times! Jesus proclaimed the Kingdom. Jesus manifested the Kingdom. Jesus modeled the Kingdom. Jesus taught the Kingdom. It is impossible to understand the ministry of Jesus apart from His commitment to the Kingdom of God. And we are forced to the unavoidable conclusion that Jesus expects that same commitment from every disciple of the Kingdom. If our message or ministry can be understood apart from the Kingdom of God, it isn't the message or ministry of Jesus.

Second, Jesus expected His disciples (and His Church) to be all about the Kingdom. *"And he called the twelve together . . . and He sent them out to proclaim the Kingdom of God."* (Luke 9:1-2) Beyond the obvious implications of the previous passage (i.e., that Jesus expected His disciples to proclaim the message of the Kingdom), how important was the Kingdom of God in Jesus' work with His disciples? Consider the following passage from the Book of Acts describing Jesus post-resurrection ministry with His disciples, *"He (Jesus) presented himself alive to them after his suffering by many proofs, appearing to them during forty*

Which Kingdom Do You Serve?

days and speaking about the Kingdom of God." (Acts 1:3) Let this sink in for a moment. Jesus regarded the message of the Kingdom as so important that He spent His last 40 days on earth after His resurrection talking to His disciples about . . . the Kingdom of God! That's important!

Did Jesus' disciples and the early Church heed the words of Jesus and carry on His message of the Kingdom? Yes they did! When we open the Book of Acts, we discover Jesus' disciples preaching the Kingdom of God where ever they went.

> *And like their Master, it is impossible to understand the ministry of the disciples and the early Church apart from their commitment to the Kingdom of God.*

*"But when they believed Philip preaching the good news about the **Kingdom of God** and the name of Jesus Christ, they were being baptized, men and women alike."* (Acts 8:12) Jesus' disciples proclaimed the Kingdom. Jesus' disciples manifested the Kingdom. Jesus' disciples modeled the Kingdom. Jesus' disciples taught the Kingdom. Just as Jesus had done for them. And like their Master, it is impossible to understand the ministry of the disciples and the early Church apart from their commitment to the Kingdom of God. The same was true of the Apostle Paul, the great "Apostle to the Gentiles." Paul proclaimed the Kingdom of God wherever he went (See Acts 14:21-22; 19:8; 20:25; 28:23), all the way to Rome: *"And he stayed two full years in his own rented quarters, and was welcoming all who came to him, preaching the **Kingdom of God**, and teaching concerning the Lord*

Secret Church

Jesus Christ with all openness." (Acts 28:30-31) Paul wasn't talking about or advocating some earthly Jewish/political Kingdom which would compete with Rome for power and position. No, Paul proclaimed a spiritual Kingdom in which Jesus, the Messiah-King, would rule the hearts and minds of men through faith. This is the Kingdom which Paul and the early Church proclaimed. And it continues to be the message of Secret Church, *"The Kingdom of God is at hand; repent, and believe the good news."*

Vanity Fair And The Kingdoms of This World

I recently had an opportunity to re-read parts of ***The Pilgrim's Progress*** by John Bunyan. In particular, I read the account of Christian and Faithful and their journey through "Vanity-Fair." This is Bunyan's allegorical description of this world - and the kingdoms of this world - where we as believers find ourselves living as "pilgrims" and "sojourners." In Bunyan's theology (which is sound biblical theology) we are all sojourners through "Vanity-Fair" on our life-journey to the Celestial City of the Kingdom of God. Bunyan writes:

"Then I saw in my dream, that when they were got out of the Wilderness, they presently saw a Town before them, and the name of that Town is Vanity, and at the Town there is a Fair kept, called Vanity-Fair: It is kept all the year long; it beareth the name of Vanity-Fair, because the Town where it is kept is lighter than Vanity; and also, because all that is there sold, or that cometh thither, is Vanity. As is the saying of the Wise, All that cometh is Vanity."

Which Kingdom Do You Serve?

Much to our collective discomfort, Bunyan's description of this world as "Vanity-Fair" is consistent with Paul's description of this world as *"this present evil age"* (Galatians 1:4). This present age began at creation, was corrupted by

> *This present age is "evil" - morally and ethically corrupt at its core - and only the return of Jesus at the end of the age will change that reality.*

mankind's fall into sin, and will conclude at "the end of the age" when Jesus returns to inaugurate "the age to come" (see Matthew 12:32; 13:39-40, 49; 24:3; 28:20). In describing this present age Paul uses the Greek word *poneros*, which refers to moral, ethical evil. This present age is "evil" - morally and ethically corrupt at its core - and only the return of Jesus at the end of the age will change that reality. As George Eldon Ladd explains, *"It is . . . basic to our understanding of the Kingdom of God to recognize the Biblical teaching that This Age is in rebellion against God's rule. The New Testament sets The Age To Come in direct opposition to This Age. The present age is evil, but the Kingdom of God belongs to The Age To Come."* [25]

As a result of this spiritual reality, we are faced with a harsh practical reality: all transformations in this present evil age are temporary, because the "spirit of the age" wars against them. The Evangelical Awakening in England under such men as George Whitefield and John and Charles Wesley,

---

[25] George Eldon Ladd, ***The Gospel Of The Kingdom***, Page 31.

Secret Church

profoundly transformed English culture and society for a hundred years (think 1750 - 1850). But today, the names of Whitefield and Wesley and their profound impact are only vague memories, while mosques are replacing Churches at an alarming rate in formerly "Christian" England.

But the Kingdom of God abides forever, and that needs to become the "hard center" of our focus. The Kingdom of God embodies God's "hard reality"

> *Secret Church is all about the Kingdom of God.*

which provides both the "hard center" of our focus as well as the framework and motivation for everything we do.

Secret Church is all about the Kingdom of God.

A Time To Reconsider

Secret Church requires each of us to reconsider and to re-focus on the Kingdom of God. In the midst of all the horror and heartache to be found in this present evil age, the Church is called to embody and manifest the Kingdom realities of redemption, forgiveness, reconciliation and perseverance in the face of evil. It is in and through the ministry of the Church, proclaiming the good news of the Kingdom and setting the captives free from the domain of darkness, that the victory of Jesus and the Kingdom over death and hell are on clear display for all to see; at least to those who aren't blinded by some other agenda. Which side of this cosmic battle for the heart and soul of this Postmodern

Which Kingdom Do You Serve?

generation do you want to be on when the history and events of this present evil age are judged? It's time to choose, between "Vanity Fair" and the Kingdom of God. It's time for Secret Church.

We need a generation of Christians who, like Jeremiah, represent moral and spiritual bronze walls in an age of moral and spiritual mud huts (see Jeremiah 15:20). We need a generation of Christians who, like Jeremiah, weep for their lost generation;

> *We need a generation of Christians who, like Jeremiah, represent moral and spiritual bronze walls in an age of moral and spiritual mud huts.*

a Postmodern generation that has lost its ability to distinguish between reality and illusion; a generation that has lost its sense of race, gender and sexuality as sacred gifts from God to be embraced, nurtured and protected; a generation that has lost its ability to see that the hope for ending violence in America (racial or otherwise) is not in eliminating guns or taking down flags, but in exposing the root of anger, bitterness, hatred and self-love which resides in every human heart and which requires that genuine spiritual transformation which only the good news of the Kingdom can bring about.

It is time for each of us to reconsider what we believe and what we are manifesting to this generation. I am disturbed and saddened to see an increasing number of professing Christians who are more passionate about attempting to fix the broken kingdoms of men than they are about proclaiming

Secret Church

and manifesting the Kingdom of God. Is your opinion concerning gun control, the Confederate flag, "evil" corporations, wall street bankers and the minimum wage the message you want to manifest and communicate to this generation? What are you manifesting to this generation? Are you manifesting liberal or conservative politics, or are you manifesting the Kingdom of God which judges all political systems and calls all men and women everywhere (and, yes, politicians, too) to repent of their sin and rebellion and to yield to the King in faith and obedience? This lost Post-Christian Postmodern generation does NOT need (and doesn't actually want) your opinion on all these things (and more I could have listed). But they desperately need the good news of the Kingdom of God which ONLY YOU can share with them. How dare you give them anything less.

Each of us will one day be remembered for something by those we leave behind. What will you be remembered for? If I am remembered at all by those I one day leave behind, I don't want to be remembered as a

> *Each of us will one day be remembered for something by those we leave behind. What will you be remembered for?*

liberal or a conservative, a Republican or a Democrat, a Libertarian or an Independent. If I am remembered at all, I want to be remembered as a disciple of the Kingdom; a worshiper of God who loved the Lord his God with all his heart, mind, soul and strength; a servant to "the least of these" who loved his neighbor as himself; and as a disciple

Which Kingdom Do You Serve?

of the Kingdom who raised up other disciples of the Kingdom. Let everything else we did be little more than forgotten footnotes. It is time for each of us to ask ourselves a very basic question concerning everything in which we are investing our time and energy: What's that got to do with the Kingdom? If you can't answer that question without engaging in some impressive mental gymnastics, you had better stop and re-think what you're doing.

It is time for Secret Church. Are you ready?

Secret Church

Chapter 6
Secret Church

"If you would make the greatest success of your life, try to discover what God is doing in your time, and fling yourself into the accomplishment of His purpose and will." - Arthur Wallis

Welcome to Secret Church, and to what God is doing in our time. Now, it's time to fling ourselves into accomplishing His purpose and will for these times. And let's begin by considering what it means to be leaders during such times.

Red Skies And Leadership

"And the Pharisees and Sadducees came, and to test him they asked him to show them a sign from heaven. He answered them, 'When it is evening, you say, 'It will be fair weather, for the sky is red.' And in the morning, 'It will be stormy today, for the sky is red and threatening.' You know how to interpret the appearance of the sky, but you cannot interpret the signs of the times.'" (Matthew 16:1-3)

Only a fool ignores the weather. That was Jesus' point. The ancient mariners had a saying that went something like this:

> *"Red sky at night, a sailor's delight;*
> *Red sky at morning, sailor take warning."*

Everyone in Jesus' day understood what He meant. Only a fool would venture out onto the water in the face of obvious

Secret Church

warnings of approaching bad weather. It wasn't just a matter of common sense. It was a matter of life and death. Within the context of

> *Spiritually blind people don't need new truths to stare at.*

Matthew 16 the meaning went even deeper: people tend to ignore the obvious signs of God's workings while demanding new signs. Jesus' response was simple but profound. Because they had ignored the obvious signs around them (healing the sick, raising the dead, casting out demons - all messianic signs of the Kingdom of God) they neither needed nor deserved any additional sign (other than the resurrection itself, which he alludes to in 16:4). Spiritually blind people don't need new truths to stare at.

Do you understand the weather of the times we are living in? These are times of great upheaval. Political upheaval. Economic upheaval. Moral collapse. Wars in the Middle East. Genocide of Christians by Muslims in Sudan and Darfur. A resurgent and militant Islam. The public persecution of politically incorrect conscience. And what if such upheavals are only the *"beginnings of birth pangs,"* the kinds of epic upheaval that Jesus said would characterize the period just before his return at the end of the age (see Matthew 24)? And if we are indeed approaching the end of the age and Jesus' soon return, then we know at least two things with a high degree of certainty, things which will affect each of us. **First**, we know that things will get progressively worse (occasionally better, but progressively worse). And, **second**, we know that "Church-as-we-have-known-it" will have to

Secret Church

change . . . dramatically! Are you prepared to lead God's Secret Church during such times?

To make things even more confusing and challenging, times of great spiritual revival and awakening often coincide with times of great cultural upheaval and even judgment. It is like standing

Are you prepared to lead God's Secret Church through times of both spiritual awakening and judgment?

at the turbulent confluence of two great rivers. On the one hand, the River of God's Spirit, the River of Ezekiel 47, will flow in great power and blessing for spiritual renewal and revival the likes of which have not been seen or experienced in the West in well over 100 years or more. On the other hand, the River of God's judgment upon our increasingly "spiritually adulterous" culture is also preparing to flow in great power. Are you prepared to lead God's Secret Church through times of both spiritual awakening and judgment?

This is "red sky" weather and it comes with a warning. This is the challenge and the urgency now facing each of us individually and the Church at large. If God is indeed raising up His end-time Church, then it will be the Church which witnesses those catastrophic events which will precede Jesus' soon return. And that means there is an urgency to our obedience. It means that time is indeed short and things are going to get much worse, and that requires a new kind of end-time Church, and a new breed of end-time leaders to lead that Church. Are you one of them? Are you ready to

Secret Church

lead God's Secret Church?

Leaders Versus Followers

"And of the sons of Issachar, men who understood the times, with knowledge of what Israel should do, their chiefs were two hundred; and all their kinsmen were at their command." (1 Chronicles 12:32)

Among the twelve tribes of Ancient Israel, the tribe of Issachar was an unlikely place to find leaders. There were far more "biblical" reasons to look for qualified leaders among such groups as the tribe of Levi (the tribe of hereditary priests, dedicated to serving God), or the tribe of Judah (from which the Messiah would come). But when "push-came-to-shove" it was the obscure tribe of Issachar which stepped up and provided leadership.

According to the last enumeration of families found in Numbers 26:25 the tribe of Issachar consisted of 64,300 "families" (probably heads of households over age 21). It's easy to count heads. There are always plenty of them to count. But when it came to numbering those from among the heads who actually understood the times and knew what Israel should do, the number quickly shrank, from 64,300 down to 200.

Followers are relatively easy to find. But finding leaders who can see and understand the "weather" of their time, who can hear from God, and who know what He is doing in their day,

Secret Church

is much more difficult. Just ask the famous sons of Issachar. The ratio there was 1 leader among every 321 followers. Which are you?

This is your call and challenge to leadership in your day. God is looking for and calling out leaders who understand "the weather," the urgency of our time, and who want to be a part of the new thing He is doing in this coming season of cultural collapse and spiritual outpouring. As America and the West plunge headlong into the Abyss of collapse and judgment, carrying much of the organized Church in-tow, are you prepared to lead God's Secret Church in a different direction? If so, then let's get started.

> *God is looking for and calling out leaders who understand "the weather."*

Organic Church

"And he said, 'The kingdom of God is as if a man should scatter seed on the ground. He sleeps and rises night and day, and the seed sprouts and grows; he knows not how. The earth produces by itself, first the blade, then the ear, then the full grain in the ear. But when the grain is ripe, at once he puts in the sickle, because the harvest has come.'" (Mark 4:26-29)

Secret Church is about the "organic" growth of the Kingdom, not its "organized" growth. Most of Culture-bound organized Christianity aims for the billboard along the freeway. Organic

Secret Church

> *Secret Church is about the "organic" growth of the Kingdom, not its "organized" growth.*

Christianity aims for the grass beneath the billboard. Over time, the billboard loses and the grass wins. The Kingdom of God is in the grass, not the billboard. If you don't understand what I just said, then you aren't ready to lead God's Secret Church.

Men create organizations to perpetuate what they are doing, while God creates organisms to reproduce what He is doing. Among the kingdoms of men, wisdom says, *"Organization is the key to success."* And because this is widely accepted wisdom we dutifully set off to form our organizations, our non-profit corporations, our 501c(3)s, and our boards of directors, thereby all but guaranteeing that, eventually, the spiritually gifted visionaries who created the organization will be ruled by the spiritually blind who want to control it. But

> *The goal of Secret Church is not to perpetuate the works of men, but to reproduce the works of God and His Kingdom.*

as the above parable from the Gospel of Mark tells us, the Kingdom of God operates on the basis of an "organic wisdom" which men cannot control, and shouldn't try. The wisdom sought by "disciples of the Kingdom" is simply to know when it is the right time to *"put in the sickle, because the harvest has come."* The goal of Secret Church is not to perpetuate the works of men, but to reproduce the works of

Secret Church

God and His Kingdom.[26]

Secret Church is an idea, not a program, a structure, an organization . . . or a billboard. It's about what it means to "be" the Church and to manifest the Kingdom of God, particularly during difficult times. Secret Church embodies what God's people have always done for 2,000 years during times of great upheaval and persecution.

It isn't possible to discuss everything you might want to know at this point. My wife and I have been involved in organic house Church (basic roots of Secret Church) for some 15 years. You will find many of the lessons we discovered and learned during our journey in our books ***River Houses Rising*** and ***Safe Houses Of Hope And Prayer***.[27] I will be mentioning these and other books we have written on this subject as we move forward in this chapter. Remember, this chapter is a beginning, not an end or a final destination. Your personal journey into Secret Church requires some intentionality on your part, and that

> *Your personal journey into Secret Church requires some intentionality on your part.*

---

[26] We treat this parable from the perspective of what it means for our discipleship in *"Lesson 40 - The Organic Growth Of The Kingdom"* of our book, ***And They Dreamt Of A Kingdom***, available via our website at risingrivermedia.org.

[27] Both of these books, along with others, are available via our website at risingrivermedia.org.

Secret Church

includes educating yourself on some of the basic questions and issues which inevitably arise. And trust me on this. We've been doing this for a while. The issues we discuss in our books will arise in your fellowship! But the mark of a genuine biblical leader is someone who understands their own call, who understands the times in which they live, and who embraces issues as they arise and seeks God for guidance and resolution for the edification (i.e., "the building up") of the Church.

No! It Isn't Time to Dig a "Hobbit Hole"

Secret Church isn't about running away, heading for the hills, building a survival compound, buying seven years worth of freeze-dried food and converting your 401K to gold and silver. So, no, it isn't time to go dig a "hobbit hole" in the false hope that your part of the Shire will survive the collapse of everything else. No. Secret Church isn't about "hunkering down." Secret Church is about reducing our entanglements and visibility to the kingdoms of this world in order to increase our effectiveness for the Kingdom of God. Secret Church is about "being" the Church and manifesting the beauty and the majesty of the Kingdom of God during difficult times. Let me offer an historical example from the life of the ancient Church.

> *Secret Church is about reducing our entanglements and visibility to the kingdoms of this world in order to increase our effectiveness for the Kingdom of God.*

Secret Church

In his wonderful book, **Water From A Deep Well**, Dr. Gerald Sittser documents how the early Church *"cared for people during periods of intense crisis."* [28] During that period when Christianity was an illegal religion and the profession of Christianity was punishable by imprisonment, torture and death (circa A.D. 65 - 313), the Roman world suffered two catastrophic plagues (the Antonine Plague [A.D.165-180] and the Plague of Cyprian [A.D. 250]) which wiped out up to one-quarter of the population during each plague (probably smallpox). Rather than running away from the dying, which is what the average Roman did, Christians did two things. Christians used their teaching and preaching to make sense of what was happening. Sittser writes,

"The plague afflicted both pagans and Christians. But the response of the two groups was decidedly different, as observers noted. The Christian worldview offered a more satisfying explanation of the disaster. Bishops in particular used their pulpits to answer the hard questions and to provide comfort and hope. They preached on such themes as God's sovereignty, the suffering of Jesus, the last judgment and the resurrection of the dead. They also interpreted the catastrophe as a kind of divine test. Cyprian, the bishop of Carthage when the plague of 250 struck, asked his congregation whether they would show the same kind of generosity to victims that God extends to the least

---

[28]Dr. Gerald L. Sittser, **Water From A Deep Well: Christian Spirituality From early Martyrs To Modern Missionaries** (Downers Grove: InterVarsity Press, 2007), page 63.

Secret Church

deserving."[29]

But Christians did more. They ran toward the dying. In the words of Dionysius, bishop of Alexandria, Christians *"showed unbounded love and loyalty, never sparing themselves and thinking only of one another. Heedless of danger, they took charge of the sick, attending to their every need and ministering to them in Christ, and with them departed this life serenely happy."* Sittser notes, *"They discovered soon enough that, however Christlike their behavior, they would not be spared from the same fate that had already taken the lives of others."* [30]

One of the greatest challenges facing the Church of our day has to do with our ability to provide balance along with a biblical perspective during times of crisis and upheaval. And we can't do that by running away and hunkering down. Secret Church is about lowering our visibility to the kingdoms of this world in order to increase our effectiveness for the Kingdom of God. Far too many professing Christians today act like they are "running for the rapture" rather than running to the battle. Where are you running?

> *Far too many professing Christians today act like they are "running for the rapture" rather than running to the battle.*

---

[29] Ibid.

[30] Sittser, page 64.

Secret Church

The Future Is Here (So, Where Are You?)

You need to know that, just as our culture's headlong plunge into the Abyss is already a reality, so too, Secret Church is already here. For some time now, while much of the Church has focused its attention on trends such as mega-Church and multi-site Church, significant numbers of professing believers have been quietly leaving the organized Church. Many of these have been the silent forerunners and pioneers of Secret Church. Christian researcher and writer George Barna states that, according to his research, four out of ten born again Christians do not attend traditional Church, and there are more than 10 million born again Christians in America alone who are not attending traditional Church. Author Reggie McNeal, Director of leadership development for the South Carolina Baptist Convention writes:

"A growing number of people are leaving the institutional Church for a new reason. They are not leaving because they have lost faith. They are leaving the Church to preserve their faith. They contend that the Church no longer contributes to their spiritual development. In fact, they say, quite the opposite. The number of "post-generational" Christians is growing. David Barrett, author of the World Christian Encyclopedia, estimates that there are about 112 million "Churchless Christians" world wide, and about 5 percent of all adherents, but he projects that number will double in the

Secret Church

next twenty five years!" [31]

My wife and I began our journey into Secret Church shortly after I completed a traditional Church pastorate. The Holy Spirit had already told us that profound changes were coming for us. He quickly led us into the organic house church movement. There we found wonderful fellowship and spiritual encouragement among hundreds of kindred spirits and fellow pilgrims whom God had also called out of traditional institutional churches. These pilgrims and pioneers were now leading organic fellowships in their homes, in coffee shops (we started ours in a Mexican Restaurant) and a wide variety of alternative locations.

Our journey into Secret Church quickly became one of the greatest (and most meaningful) challenges of our Christian lives up to that point. God called us to live by faith (I was working two jobs at the time) and to trust

> *. . . the fruit of the Kingdom grows wherever the seed of the Kingdom is sown.*

Him for our provision without any visible means of support. Little did we know that season would last for the next 15 years! Next he called us to minister in one of the poorest and most challenging neighborhoods of our city. We did Secret Church in front yards at neighborhood outreaches, sponsored block parties, fed the hungry, rescued young

---

[31] Reggie McNeal, ***The Present Future: Six Tough Questions for the Church*** (San Francisco: John Wiley & Sons, 2003), page 4.

Secret Church

mothers and children fleeing domestic violence and drugs, sheltered the homeless, learned to love the "unlovable" and to serve "the least of these."[32] God taught, and we discovered, that the fruit of the Kingdom grows wherever the seed of the Kingdom is sown; no church building or billboard required. In short, we learned what it means to "be" the Church and to make disciples of the Kingdom by walking alongside others on their spiritual journeys. And we aren't alone. Along the way we have met a growing "network" of people and groups who are already pioneering and practicing Secret Church.

❑ Paul and Lori, who lead a marriage ministry, and travel the country in their fifth-wheel, sowing the seed of the Kingdom and encouraging Secret Church;

❑ A former attorney and real estate developer from Hawaii who, along with his wife, has been part of a Secret Church network on Maui and is now building a Christian retreat ministry in Virginia to serve troubled teens and to raise up the next generation of Secret Church leaders;

❑ The Summit Fellowships, a network of organic house Churches which have been pioneering Secret Church in the Portland, Oregon area now for 25 years;

---

[32]Read more of our story in Chapter 8 of our book, ***The Least Of These: The Role Of Good Deeds In A Jesus-Shaped Spirituality***, available via our website at risingrivermedia.org.

Secret Church

- Jim and Kathy Mellon, who serve a network of house Churches in and around Killeen, Texas. Since 1992 this network has contributed more than $1,000,000 to the work of the Kingdom around the world.

- John White, a former traditional Church pastor who now leads the "Luke 10 Community" and helps equip leaders (like you!) to make disciples and to practice organic Church;

- Dyrek and Blanca, a home-schooling family who practice organic Church in central Kansas;

- And thousands more who go unnamed and unrecognized, people whom God is calling out of traditional Church structures, who practice "organic Church" and are pioneers in Secret Church. Are you one of them?

8 Commitments You Must Make

To be a genuine leader in Secret Church requires a greater-than-average degree of intentionality and discernment on our part. We live in a highly distracted age. The latest viral "Tweet" or Facebook post or YouTube

> *To be a genuine leader in Secret Church requires a greater-than-average degree of intentionality and discernment on our part.*

Secret Church

video and people around the world are glued to their smart phones. Yep, it's like shouting "squirrel" to a pack of curious canines. So many things - some good, some not so good - loudly compete for our attention. This is true of things outside the Church in our larger culture; but it is also true of things inside the culture of the Church. Hardly a day goes by that I don't receive at least one "must see video" in my e-mail inbox from some ministry hoping that my curiosity will get the best of me and I'll watch their latest video production (which NEVER turns out to be a "must see"). I've learned to delete first and ask questions later. Sorry, but I have to be intentional in what I do and I simply don't have time to get distracted. And neither do you. Students of philosophy are familiar with a declaration made by the Ancient Greek philosopher, Socrates, that the unexamined life is not worth living (Plato's *Apology*, 38). How much more should we as Christians examine our lives, we upon whom *"the end of the ages has come"* (1 Corinthians 10:11). It is time for each of us to examine our spiritual lives and our priorities. When it comes to practicing Secret Church, intentionality requires that you and I identify our priorities and make some specific commitments which will guide us in our decision-making as we move forward. I want to offer a brief list of some basic commitments that each of us needs to make in order to succeed as leaders of Secret Church.

> *It is time for each of us to examine our spiritual lives and our priorities.*

Secret Church

1. A Commitment To Stop Chasing "Squirrels" - Yes, I'm repeating myself. Got it. But living as part of a culture which increasingly demonstrates the attention span of a gnat and the commitment level of a curious canine, this really is important and bears repeating. Without a personal commitment to exercise discernment and to not get distracted by every wind of doctrine and every latest cultural craze, it won't be long before you will be off chasing the latest political "messiah," the latest prophetic worship craze, the latest gold dust meeting or manna meeting or gemstone meeting or angelic manifestation or (feel free to fill-in-the-blank at this point with your favorite) some other distraction. I've personally witnessed and/or experienced all of these and more. If it isn't the Kingdom, why are you chasing it? If it doesn't enable you to make disciples, why are you chasing it? If it doesn't equip you to serve "the least of these," why are you chasing it? Each of us must identify and come to terms with our own personal "squirrels" (we ALL have them. What's yours?) and make a conscious commitment to stop chasing them . . . or to pay the price. And there is always a price to be paid for distracted living and chasing squirrels.

> *If it isn't the Kingdom, why are you chasing it? If it doesn't enable you to make disciples, why are you chasing it?*

2. A Commitment To "Be" The Church - The motto of Secret Church is, *"We don't go to Church; we ARE the Church."* This phrase has received a fair amount of attention

Secret Church

> *No great structure can survive the collapse of the values which created it. It is true of civilizations. It is also true of Churches.*

in recent years, even being frequently repeated in traditional, institutional Church contexts. But the phrase reflects something much deeper than most people understand: the difference between "structure" on the one hand, and "values" on the other hand. I said earlier in this book that *"great civilizations collapse first at the margins because the center can no longer hold them together."* To state this truth another way, when the structures of great civilizations collapse, it is because the values which built and supported those structures collapsed much earlier. No great structure can survive the collapse of the values which created it. It is true of civilizations. It is also true of Churches.

To "go to Church" is to emphasize the importance of "structure"; to "be the Church" is to emphasize the importance of "values." Do you understand the difference? "Values" reproduce; "structures" perpetuate. Do you understand the difference? Secret Church emphasizes "values" over "structure." I talk about this difference in greater depth in two of our books. First, in *"Chapter 4 - Honey, I Shrunk The Church"* of our book **Safe Houses of Hope and Prayer** I include a chart entitled *"Comparing Values"* (on page 47) which compares the difference between seventeen (17) values of "organic Church" versus "institutional Church." I would strongly encourage you to get a copy of that book.

Secret Church

Second, in *"Chapter 8 - The Things That Shape Us"* of our book **And They Dreamt Of A Kingdom**, I discuss in detail how our structures shape us and eventually prevent us from doing the very things Jesus commanded us to do, including making disciples who embody the values of the Kingdom.

A commitment to Secret Church embodies a commitment to embrace the values of the Kingdom of God. This is about more than understanding a *"Comparing Values"* chart. It's about embracing the transforming power of the Kingdom toward everything it touches, and it's about living out the "inverted" values of the Kingdom which are foolishness in the eyes of this world.[33] It took Jesus just over three years to impart these values to His disciples. Why do we think it will take us less time to impart those same values to those whom we disciple? Discipleship isn't about teaching people how to run our Church programs or maintain our Church structure. In the Kingdom of God, discipleship is about imparting values, not information. But once those values have been imparted, they are transferable to any situation we may find ourselves in. We carry our values with us wherever we go. We take those values into homeless

> *A commitment to Secret Church embodies a commitment to embrace the values of the Kingdom of God.*

---

[33] Again, we discuss the values of the Kingdom in greater depth in our book, **And They Dreamt Of A Kingdom: Biblical Studies In Discipleship And The Kingdom Of God**, available via our website at risingrivermedia.org

Secret Church

shelters, into food banks, into shelters for women fleeing domestic violence and the sex trafficking trade. In other words, we take the values of the Kingdom into our personal discipleship and we express

> *In the Kingdom of God, discipleship is about imparting values, not information.*

them as we serve others in the name of Jesus. And THAT is what it means to "be" the Church.

3. A Commitment To Go Small . . . And Go Home - Not too long ago a conference was held at an Evangelical denominational mega-Church with a large campus on the outskirts of Raleigh, North Carolina (where my older brother has been involved for several years, which is how I know about what took place). The speakers included well known denominational leaders who delivered a sobering message. Significant changes are coming, and it's time to begin thinking about how to shed your large buildings. In short, your structures must change. The big must become small, and the complex must be made simple (which is where the idea of "Simple Church" originated).

This will be a serious challenge for those Churches which have allowed their structure to shape their ministries and to determine their values. Those large buildings are about to become both a burden and a target. But turning the Titanic is harder than it looks or sounds. You're plunging headlong into an ice field with a ship that's moving too fast for conditions, that's too big for its rudder and not enough

Secret Church

lifeboats for half the passengers. Apart from those realities, life's good. So, how do you down-size your mega-Church when you have a congregation of some 3,000 people supporting a campus with $10 million of debt (and a recent debt-retirement campaign which flopped!)?

The same denomination recently announced that it would soon be laying off hundreds of foreign missionaries because giving for missions has been declining for several

> *. . . structural collapse at the margins occurs because values at the core have already collapsed.*

years and they can no longer make up the difference from reserve funds (in other words, they've already waited too long). Again, even in the Church, structural collapse at the margins occurs because values at the core have already collapsed. And that collapse demands that we reconsider our American obsession with size.

American culture is obsessed with "size." We have an absolute love-fetish for things which are big. Big equals important. Big equals successful. This includes how we measure success in the Church. We measure success by the size of our building or campus, the size of our congregation and the size of our budget (including our missions budget). Big is good. Big equals success. Big also equals effective. No questions asked. While we could spend considerable time here questioning each of these assumptions, there is little need to do so. The looming collapse of our civilization -

Secret Church

both inside and outside the Church - is about to make all such discussions moot. As our civilization plunges headlong into the approaching Abyss, "big" will no longer offer either success or safety. In fact, "big" is about to become both a burden and a target (Re-read Chapter 2 if you don't understand what that means) for those who cling to its allure. Rather, we are entering into a new season in which "small is the new big" (I discuss this in *"Chapter 14 - Rabbits, Elephants And Mules"* of **River Houses Rising**).[34]

Let's stop for just a moment and "run the numbers." Let's pretend for just a moment that you presently attend a "small" mega-Church of only 2,000 people (the minimum definition of "mega-Church"). I would be willing to wager that you don't know more than 15-25 people in the Church. By "know" I mean that you and your family actually interact with them and their family outside of whatever services you attend; praying together, hanging out together, working through life's issues together. Now, there's a reason for this. Among a group of 15 people there are no less than 225 possible lines of communication. Among a larger group of 25 people that number rises to 625. In other words, meaningful communication begins to break down once any group grows beyond 15 people. At 25 people, you really are "maxed out." To put this in simple terms, your circle of meaningful relationships in your mega-Church fellowship (or ANY

---

[34]On the topic of going small, I highly recommend Tony and Felicity Dale, ***The Rabbit and the Elephant: Why Small Is the New Big for Today's Church*** (Carol Stream, Illinois: Tyndale House Publishers, 2009).

Secret Church

Church fellowship, for that matter) is between 15 and 25 people; about the size of a healthy organic house Church.

Now, traditional Churches are not clueless to this reality. Many of them have attempted to address this issue by creating what is known as a "small group" ministry.

> *Secret Church is NOT another "small group."*

But in spite of an entire curriculum industry devoted to promoting and supporting these small groups, most of these groups fail. Why? Primarily due to a lack of purpose, focus or vision beyond the group. They don't really know why they are there. Believers today are so accustomed to having a program, and someone to lead and spoon-feed them, that they don't have a clue about how to "be" the Church without someone to tell them what to do. They have no personal or group vision for where God may be taking them. As a result, their "small group" has simply become a "small box" inside a "large box." Such groups never learn how to worship together; they never make disciples; they never learn to serve "the least of these"; they never reproduce; they never grow beyond being a therapeutic extension of the organization. They never become Secret Church. In the words of one pastor, most Churches should euthanize their small groups and put them out of their misery.[35]

---

[35] See Brian Jones article *"Why Churches Should Euthanize Small Groups"* analyzing the failure of most Church-sponsored "small group" ministries. Online at http://christianstandard.com/

Secret Church

Secret Church is NOT another "small group." Secret Church is about believers becoming genuine disciples of the Kingdom and the leaders God has called and gifted them to be. Secret Church is about disciples of the Kingdom making other disciples of the Kingdom, both by instruction and example. Secret Church is about each of us discovering our call to serve "the least of these," and to manifest the values of the Kingdom of God where ever God happens to take us. Secret Church is about discovering the power of "going small" and becoming the Church which meets in YOUR house, or where ever God happens to place us.

4. A Commitment To Focus On Basics - As our civilization and culture plunge headlong into the Abyss we discussed earlier, you and I will be increasingly challenged concerning what we believe and how we practice those beliefs. If you are not clear concerning the basics of your faith, what you

It's time to focus on basics, and to know what you believe.

believe and why you believe it, and how to gather with others who share your beliefs as a Secret Church, you will become a disoriented, and confused spiritual casualty of the Abyss. Remember, there's a reason why Jesus warned His disciples, *". . . when the Son of Man comes, will he find faith on earth?"* (Luke 18:8). As this plunge into the Abyss unfolds, your faith, obedience and discipleship will be tested beyond anything you have ever known or experienced. It's

Secret Church

time to focus on basics, and to know what you believe. [36]

Secret Church is about focusing on the basics and *"keeping the main thing the main thing."* When it comes to matters of faith, Church and spirituality, what is "the main thing"? If someone were to ask you for "the main thing" in biblical Christianity - in your personal faith - could you tell

> *As this plunge into the Abyss unfolds, your faith, obedience and discipleship will be tested beyond anything you have ever known or experienced.*

them in 50 words or less? Your ability to answer that question demonstrates your ability (or your inability) to focus on basics. Consider this answer: *"Jesus is Lord, God and King; the Kingdom of God is at hand; the resurrection of Jesus is the proof; the outpouring of the Holy Spirit on the Day of Pentecost is the sign that we are living in the "last days"; Jesus is coming again soon. Repent, and believe the good news."* Is there more to biblical Christianity than that simple declaration (O.K., simple as in 55 words!). Of course there is, and I have a shelf filled with excellent systematic theology books to prove it! But when Christians and Christianity are persecuted by the world, it usually isn't over their systematic theology. It's over their basic profession of

---

[36] I recommend two books to help you focus on basics: Paul Little, ***Know What You Believe*** (Downers Grove: IVP Books, 2008), and J. I. Packer, ***Concise Theology: A Guide To Historic Christian Beliefs*** (Carol Stream: Tyndale House Publishers, 2001). Know what is critical and what is not.

Secret Church

faith, and how that profession manifests itself in their daily lives.

The best example of this is the experience of the early Church from the time of the Emperor Nero (A.D. 54-68) until the time of the Emperor Diocletian (A.D. 284-305). During that time Christianity was a prohibited religion and the profession of Christianity was punishable by arrest, imprisonment, torture and death. When accused Christians were brought before the Roman magistrates they were traditionally given an opportunity to prove their innocence and to recant their faith by offering a pinch of sacrificial incense at an altar to the Roman Emperor while declaring, *"Caesar is Lord."* Why this declaration? Because it was the exact opposite of the basic declaration of faith in the early Church: *"Jesus is Lord."*

All of this serves to highlight a critical issue. What are the essential basics of our faith which cannot be compromised under any circumstances, but must be "held fast" regardless the price. Whenever Christians and the Church are persecuted, there is almost always a *"Caesar is Lord versus Jesus is Lord"* moment involved. It may come disguised as a confrontation over same sex marriage or abortion or some other issue of

> *Whenever Christians and the Church are persecuted, there is almost always a "Caesar is Lord versus Jesus is Lord" moment involved.*

Secret Church

biblical obedience and/or faith, but at its heart it is a confrontation over where the faith and loyalty of the Christian ultimately lies. Our Post-Christian, Postmodern culture really doesn't care whether you are a Calvinist or an Arminian; whether you are pre-trib or post-trib; whether you are a Republican or a Democrat. But our Post-Christian, Postmodern culture demands to know if you and I are "fully on board" with their plunge into the Abyss. Failure to declare anything less than "Caesar is Lord" will be met with . . . unpleasantness. One of the underlying issues at such times involves what it means to "compromise" our faith as opposed to what it means to "hold fast what you have."[37]

5. A Commitment To Serve "The Least of These" - Who are you serving? Biblical faith has always been at its best and most powerful when it is a counter-cultural witness, serving others and manifesting the values of the Kingdom. Biblical Christianity has nearly always been at its worst and most spiritually impotent when seeking to rule over others.

Earlier in this Chapter I talked about how the early Church ministered to those in need in spite of living during a time when the very profession of Christianity was punishable by imprisonment, torture and death. The early Christians were known for both their morality and their compassion. As we

---

[37] Compromise in the face of "tribulation" (i.e., overwhelming pressure) is one of the dominant issues which confronted the seven Churches of Asia in Revelation 2-3. It is a timeless and timely issue. See our book, ***When Jesus Visits His Church: Studies In The Seven Churches of Asia (Revelation 2-3)*** available via our website at risingrivermedia.org.

Secret Church

described earlier, when plague swept through the City of Rome and officials fled to the country, Christians remained behind and cared for the sick and dying. It was the Christians who searched the hills and bridges of Rome to find and rescue abandoned babies (a practice known as "exposure") and to raise them as their own.

> *As Roman civilization collapsed, it fell to Christians and the Church to pick up the pieces, to offer a comprehensive worldview and to minister to those in need, while providing encouragement and hope.*

In the mid-4th Century, the Roman Emperor Julian (A.D. 361-363, known as "Julian, the Apostate" for his rejection of Christianity and his attempts to revive Rome's ancient religions) complained to a confident, *"The impious Galileans support not only their poor, but ours as well, everyone can see that our people lack aid from us."*[38] As Roman civilization collapsed, it fell to Christians and the Church to pick up the pieces, to offer a comprehensive worldview and to minister to those in need, while providing encouragement and hope. Welcome to Secret Church.

The importance of Christians manifesting the power of the Kingdom of God by serving those in need (people whom Jesus referred to as "the least of these" in Matthew 25:40, 45) cannot be over stated. It is so important that I have

---

[38]Sittser, ***Water From A Deep Well***, page 56.

written two books on the subject. The first is entitled ***The Least of These: The Role of Good Deeds In A Jesus-Shaped Spirituality***. This book is the product of our own personal experiences of working among the homeless and marginalized over a ten-year period, and will answer many of your questions (find it on our website at risingrivermedia.org). The second book is entitled ***30 Days And 30 Ways Of Doing Good: Your Daily Guide To Greater Kindness And Good Deeds***. This is a daily action/devotional guide designed to introduce you to a wide variety of issues, along with a daily devotional thought and suggested opportunities to get personally involved. Discover what it means to manifest the values of the Kingdom by serving others in the name of Jesus!

6. A Commitment To Make Disciples - Are you a follower of Jesus, or are you a disciple? And do you know the difference? Jesus had many followers, but few disciples, as we discover in John Chapter 2, *"Now when he was in Jerusalem at the Passover Feast, many believed in his name when they saw the signs that he was doing. But Jesus on his part did not entrust himself to them, because he knew all people and needed no one to bear witness about man, for he himself knew what was in man"* (John 2:23-25). Throughout His three-and-one-half years of ministry, Jesus' focus was always upon His disciples; not upon those who followed Him. He would preach to the masses, deliver them from demonic oppression, heal their diseases and feed them when they were hungry. But Jesus' focus in every lesson and ministry activity was always upon His disciples. And His

Secret Church

parting words to those who were present at His ascension constituted a command, *"As you are going, make disciples."*

For the Church of Jesus, discipleship is a command, not an option. And yet, in spite of this background (and more we could discuss), the contemporary Church in America and the West focuses nearly all of its time, attention and resources on gathering followers rather than making disciples. The working assumption (which neither Jesus nor the early Church would understand or share) seems to be that whoever assembles on Sunday morning is a disciple by virtue of their presence.

> *For the Church of Jesus, discipleship is a command, not an option.*

As our culture plunges headlong into the approaching moral and spiritual Abyss, dragging much of the confused and compliant Church along with it, being an uncommitted "follower" of Jesus will come at an increasing price that many (if not most) will be unwilling to pay. Compromise amidst persecution and difficult times will thin the ranks of "followers" and will separate followers from disciples. Each of us who profess faith in Christ will be confronted with the question of what it really means to be a "disciple of the Kingdom" and to walk in a Jesus-shaped spirituality in the midst of moral and spiritual collapse.

> *Secret Church requires disciples, not fans or followers.*

Secret Church

Secret Church requires disciples, not fans or followers. And it's time to decide which you really are. In the days which lie ahead, each of us who claim to take our faith in Christ seriously will find ourselves increasingly challenged to answer four critical questions: 1) What is the difference between being a follower of Jesus and being a "disciple of the Kingdom"; 2) Am I a follower or a disciple; 3) How do I obey the command of Jesus to make disciples; and 4) Who am I discipling. These are the issues of Secret Church. This issue of biblical discipleship and answering these four questions is so important that we are in the process of creating a three volume set of discipleship books entitled,

Secret Church is about discipleship, not attendance.

And They Dreamt Of A Kingdom: Biblical Studies In Discipleship And The Kingdom Of God (Volume 1 is currently available via our website at risingrivermedia.org). In these books we examine every discipleship lesson Jesus taught His disciples in the chronological order and context in which He taught them. We discover the same lessons they learned and focus on how we can embrace those same lessons in our own discipleship. We learn along side the disciples what it means to be a "disciple of the Kingdom." We have written it in a format which can be used both for personal study and devotions, and as a group discipleship study for your Secret Church, or as a one-on-one discipleship study for someone you are discipling (taking one lesson per week, there is nearly one year's worth of studies in Volume 1 alone). These books provide you with a tool to accomplish

Secret Church

two key goals: 1) to help you better understand what it means to be "a disciple of the Kingdom," and 2) to provide you with what you need to disciple someone else (either individually, or in a group setting). Secret Church is about discipleship, not attendance.

7. A Commitment To Live Simply, Trust God And Invest In Eternity - I recently received an e-mail from a friend who has been a foreign missionary with a major Evangelical denomination for nearly 30 years. His denomination just announced that they would be eliminating 600 missionaries. He and his wife were being offered an early retirement package which would terminate their mission. After careful prayer they chose to accept the financial settlement, but to continue their mission on their own and trust God to meet their needs. Welcome to the future, including the future of Secret Church. Welcome to what it means to be a "disciple of the Kingdom."

Speaking to the *Society of American Newspaper Editors* in Washington, D.C. on January 17, 1925, four years before the great stock market crash of 1929, President Calvin Coolidge famously declared *"the chief business of the American people is business."* While historians have used this statement to deride Coolidge for being a one-dimensional lackey for big business interests (which he was not), the reality is that his declaration is an accurate expression of the spirit of our age (probably more so now than in Coolidge's day!). Modern business in our Post-Christian, Postmodern age loves money and loathes ethics. Major schools of

Secret Church

business around the country have all but abandoned any pretense of teaching business "ethics" because, as Harvard University admitted, they have no clue how to do so in a Postmodern age.[39] We live in an age which has concluded that economic and financial prosperity represent the "greater good" which must be separated from anything resembling ethics and morality, and certainly from anything resembling religious convictions, if such things impede "the greater good." For

> *Money and prosperity equals lifestyle and comfort. Even in Church.*

its part, the Church has allowed this "spirit of the age" to go unchallenged except for the occasional "Christian money management" workshop, while at the same time embracing the two "terrible values" of *"personal peace and personal prosperity"* which Dr. Francis Schaeffer warned us against 35 years ago. Business success and economic prosperity equals a comfortable lifestyle, even if it comes at the expense of morality, ethics and spirituality. Money and prosperity equals lifestyle and comfort. Even in Church.[40]

---

[39] See our article *"And That's Why Harvard Can't Teach Ethics,"* Appendix B in our book **30 Days And 30 Ways Of Doing Good**, available on our website at risingrivermedia.org

[40] No culture can survive without "rules" concerning right and wrong. Our Post-Christian Postmodern culture has substituted "legal" for "moral" in the hope that no one will notice. From abortion to gay marriage, if something is "legal," it is now "moral," and any dissent by a religiously informed private conscience will not be tolerated. Government has now replaced God as the arbiter of morality. 535 Congressmen and 9 Supreme Court Justices are now your moral guide and authority. Enjoy.

Secret Church

But our culture's plunge into the Abyss will change all of that. An economic prosperity built upon a foundation of Judeo-Christian ethics (such as a concern for the poor and the marginalized, concerns which Rome and the ancient world never possessed until Christianity introduced them) cannot and will not survive the loss of that foundation. And when it collapses, how will we respond? Perhaps we could learn something from the response of the Church in 1857.

In late September of 1857, banks in New York City began to see the first signs of what was then called a "banker's panic." Banks in Philadelphia had begun calling in loans and suspending payment of gold for notes. By early October the *New York Observer* was warning of *"the financial panic of 1857."* Then, on October 14, 1857, the entire banking system of the United States collapsed, bankrupting many businesses and bringing financial ruin to hundreds of thousands of people in New York, Philadelphia, Boston and other financial and industrial centers. Banks in New York would remain closed for two months. Thousands of people became unemployed and riots broke out in major cities. At the height of the crisis, the New York Synod of the Presbyterian Church published the following declaration in the *New York Observer*:

"In view of the recent commercial disaster that has come upon our country, the Synod of New York, deeply impressed by the fact that the Lord has a controversy with His people, and that it is incumbent on them to humble themselves beneath His hand, does solemnly recommend to all its

Secret Church

Churches to set apart Thursday, November 5th as a day of special humiliation and prayer to Almighty God that He will have mercy upon us." [41]

The response of the Church to the financial panic of 1857 was to declare a season of seeking God in fasting and prayer and to humble themselves in genuine introspection and repentance. God's response to the Church was to send the great Manhattan Prayer Revival of 1857. There are lessons to be learned from such things. At all times, and in all places, God is more concerned with our obedience, our holiness and our character (i.e., Christ-likeness) than he is with our lifestyle, our prosperity or our comfort. Any lifestyle (whether prosperity or poverty) God grants to the Christian is given for the sake of the Kingdom of God. If you are pursuing a financial lifestyle tied to the on-going prosperity of a culture in the throes of collapse, especially without regard to the Kingdom of God and His purposes for what He has given you, you are in trouble. It is time (past time, actually) to ask yourself some tough questions, beginning with: *"Which lifestyle am I pursuing; my lifestyle here and now which, at*

> *At all times, and in all places, God is more concerned with our obedience, our holiness and our character than he is with our lifestyle, our prosperity or our comfort.*

---

[41] See J. Edwin Orr, **The Event Of The Century: The 1857-1858 Awakening** (Wheaton, IL: International Awakening Press, 1989), page 19.

Secret Church

best, is temporary and fleeting, or my promised lifestyle in the Age to Come which is eternal?"

The values of the Kingdom (including economic values) are quite different from those of this present evil age, and go far beyond "tithing" and paying off your mortgage. As our culture plunges headlong into the coming Abyss, the conflict between the Kingdom of God and this preset evil age - between the domain of darkness and the Kingdom of God's Son (Colossians 1:13) - will intensify and every genuine "disciple of the Kingdom" will be forced to answer three basic "financial" questions:

Question # 1 - Who Are You Trusting To Meet Your Needs? We live in an age, a culture and a generation which have been taught to look to politicians and government to meet their needs. From health care to Social Security retirement, from gun violence to gay marriage, from race relations to economic "justice" and much more, we have been brainwashed to "believe" that more government is the answer . . . whatever the question or need might be. But there is a price to be paid for such "idolatry." In the Church, we pay the price by witnessing the rise of a generation of professing Christians who go through the motions of "trusting God" but who are spiritually bankrupt when it comes to the reality of living by faith in times of genuine crisis. This situation was eloquently described a generation ago by pastor and author A.W. Tozer:

"Many of us Christians have become extremely skillful in

Secret Church

arranging our lives so as to admit the truth of Christianity without being embarrassed by its implications. We arrange things so that we can get on well enough without divine aid, while at the same time ostensibly seeking it. We boast in the Lord but watch carefully that we never get caught depending on Him. . . . Pseudo faith always arranges a way out to serve in case God fails it. Real faith knows only one way and gladly allows itself to be stripped of any second way or makeshift substitutes. For true faith, it is either God or total collapse . . . . What we need very badly these days is a company of Christians who are prepared to trust God as completely now as they know they must do at the last day. For each of us the time is coming when we shall have nothing but God. Health and wealth and friends and hiding places will be swept away and we shall have only God. To the man of pseudo faith that is a terrifying thought, but to real faith it is one of the most comforting thoughts the heart can entertain." [42]

For the Christian, the issue of trusting God for our needs is as old as the Gospels. This issue lay at the heart of Jesus' ministry with His disciples, and particularly with regard to their call to follow Him, found in Luke 5:1-11. In order to truly move forward in their discipleship with Jesus, His disciples had to confront and overcome their servile (i.e., "slavish") fears concerning how their needs would be met. They had to come to a point of realization and genuine trust that the God Who could fill their fishing boats with fish, to the point of

---

[42] A. W. Tozer, ***The Root Of The Righteous*** (Camp Hill, PA: Wing Spread Publishers, 2006), page 52.

Secret Church

sinking, could be trusted to meet their need for fish . . . and more. *"And when they had brought their boats to land, they left everything and followed him."* (Luke 5:11)[43]

There is nothing wrong with hard work, prudent planning or taking a government benefit for which you may qualify. Yes, there may be times when God meets your needs through food stamps or unemployment compensation or subsidized health care.

The problem arises when the object of our trust for meeting our needs shifts away from God and to something else.

The problem arises when the object of our trust for meeting our needs shifts away from God and to something else. At that moment idolatry is born, and the servile fear of losing our "benefits" replaces trust in God's ability to care for us.

As our culture plunges headlong into the approaching Abyss and governments are increasingly unable to fulfill their promises to the masses who trusted them, how will you respond? Will you join the masses in panic and unbelief? At that moment you will discover the true object of your faith, and the truth of Jesus' words, *"No one can serve two masters, for either he will hate the one and love the other, or he will be devoted to the one and despise the other. You*

---

[43]We treat this passage at length in *"Lesson 19 - Do Not Be Afraid"* in ***And They Dreamt Of A Kingdom, Volume 1***, available via our website at risingrivermedia.org.

Secret Church

cannot serve God and money." (Matthew 6:24)

Question # 2 - Who Are You Living For? Earlier in this section I made the statement that money and prosperity equals lifestyle and comfort. Even in Church. Our lifestyle - how we spend the resources God has given us - is the truest expression of our financial priorities and a genuine indicator of who we are living for. My favorite story which illustrates this point comes from the life of John Wesley, founder of the Methodist Church and leader the Evangelical Awakening in England in the 1700s. In the year 1776, John Wesley received a note from the Commissioner of Excise. At that time the British Government raised tax revenue by imposing a luxury excise tax upon all silver plate (sterling silver dinnerware, etc.). The Commissioner of Excise claimed that Wesley owned more silver plate than he had declared and paid tax on. Wesley responded curtly but profoundly, *"I have two silver spoons at London and two at Bristol. This is all the plate I have at present, and I shall not buy any more while so many round me want bread."* Is it any wonder that Wesley never heard back from the Commissioner of Excise? It's hard to argue with the eloquence of a Jesus-shaped spirituality which understands that our lifestyle embodies both our financial priorities and our commitment to serve others and the

> *Our lifestyle . . . is the truest expression of our financial priorities and a genuine indicator of who we are living for.*

Secret Church

Kingdom of God.[44]

Question # 3 - What Is Your True Stewardship? The concepts of "stewardship" (Greek: *oikonomia*, literally, "household management") and of being a "steward" (Greek: *oikonomos*, literally, "manager of a household") are well known metaphors in the New Testament. Unfortunately, too much of the Church has reduced "stewardship" to an exercise in financial accounting, bookkeeping and giving. In the New Testament, the primary biblical application of "stewardship" is not financial but spiritual. The Apostle Paul tells us that we are "stewards" of the gospel and the truths of the Kingdom, *"This is how one should regard us, as servants of Christ and stewards of the mysteries of God. Moreover, it is required of stewards that they be found faithful."* (1 Corinthians 4:1-2). In two simple-but-profound verses Paul sums up the heart of biblical stewardship: faithfulness in our management of "the mysteries of God." The Apostle Peter adds another dimension when he instructs believers, *"As each has received a gift, use it to serve one another, as good stewards of God's varied grace"* (1 Peter 4:10). Peter reminds us of the

> . . . too much of the Church has reduced "stewardship" to an exercise in financial accounting, bookkeeping and giving.

---

[44] For more on Wesley, the topic of money and lifestyle and our personal journey into living by faith, see *"Chapter 2 - Who Do I Make My Check Out To - Part 2"* in our book **Safe Houses Of Hope And Prayer**, available via our website at risingrivermedia.org.

Secret Church

importance of personal faithfulness in using the spiritual gifts God has given us to serve one another in the community of believers. That, too, is biblical "stewardship."

Who are you trusting to meet your needs; God or someone (or something) else? What does your lifestyle say about your spiritual and financial priorities? What is the focus of your "stewardship"? Is your stewardship an exercise in good accounting and shrewd investing, or an expression of your commitment to a more simplified lifestyle for the sake of sowing into the Kingdom and the lives of others. As Randy Alcorn likes to say, we may not be able to take it with us, but we can send it on ahead by investing wisely in the work of the Kingdom here and now. As a rule, I do not "invest" in programs or buildings. I prefer to sow into the lives of people, their needs, their ministry for the Kingdom and their vision for serving others. Where are you sowing?

8. A Commitment To Fast And Pray For Spiritual Awakening

Twenty years ago I wrote a history of the great Welsh Revival of 1904. One of the people at the heart of that

> *"Bend the Church, save the world."*

spiritual outpouring was a young 26 year old former coal miner named Evan Roberts. In the course of the revival Roberts declared, *"Bend the Church, save the world."* As a theologian and amateur historian of revival movements, I believe the greatest obstacle to the salvation of the nations

Secret Church

is an unbent, unholy and unrepentant Church which loves itself, its opinions, its programs and its lifestyle more than it loves either perishing men or the Kingdom of God. At the end of the day, how much we genuinely love God, love perishing men and how much we long for the spiritual revival of the Church and the awakening of the masses to faith and salvation, will be reflected in our own commitment to fast and pray for these things. What's your commitment?

The history of revivals and spiritual awakenings over the past 300 years strongly suggests that such spiritual outpourings do not come to those who simply want them or occasionally ask for them. They come for two primary reasons. First, they come because somewhere there existed a person or a group of people who were willing to pay the price of intense and prolonged fasting and intercession; like John Knox, crying out, *"Great God, give me Scotland or I shall die."* Second, they come because God in His Sovereignty chooses to send them in response to the cry of His people, and in a desire to renew His Church and extend His Kingdom. I believe that the next great movement of God's Spirit in revival and spiritual awakening will begin in, and move through, organic Secret Churches, gathering in places ranging from private homes to homeless shelters where disciples of the Kingdom are worshiping, sowing the seed of the Kingdom and serving those in need.

Getting Started

"And day by day continuing with one mind in the temple, and

Secret Church

breaking bread from house to house, they were taking their meals together with gladness and sincerity of heart, praising God, and having favor with all the people. And the Lord was adding to their number day by day those who were being saved" (Acts 2:46-47).

When the Church was born in the Book of Acts, beginning at Pentecost, those early disciples had no idea how to "do" Church. Like you, they had NEVER "done" Secret Church, or any other kind of Church gathering. But by Acts Chapter 7, after a span of only a few weeks, those early disciples had recognized gifted leaders, assigned responsibilities according to gifts, callings and needs and organized thousands of new converts into a network of organic house churches, spread out all over Jerusalem. These "Secret Churches" met regularly from house-to-house, shared meals together and shared resources to help those in need (read the first seven chapters of Acts to get the whole picture). What is truly amazing, by modern "church growth" standards, is that they did it all without a budget, a building, a professionally trained staff, any "how to" manuals, any church planting or church growth workshops, and no worship team. And they did it all while enduring persecution, first from institutional Judaism and later from Rome itself. It was Simple Church. It was Organic Church. It was Secret Church. It later became an

Secret Church

Underground Church. But most importantly, it was Effective Church, effective for the times in which they lived. How effective? So effective that they were accused of turning the Mediterranean world upside down (see Acts 17:6).

There's an important point here. Secret Church isn't about a program. Secret Church is a lifestyle; a lifestyle of being a disciple of the Kingdom, lived out in community with other disciples of the Kingdom. That was true of Secret Church in the 1st Century, and it is true of Secret Church today. It is somewhat ironic that as our civilization collapses and devolves into that same moral and spiritual paganism which characterized ancient Rome, God is calling His Church back to being the counter-cultural witness of 1st Century Secret Church. Your journey into Secret Church truly begins when you and I embrace the biblical truth that we don't "go" to Church. We "are" the Church, a small manifestation of the Kingdom of God where ever we happen to be, starting in our homes.

> *Secret Church isn't about a program. Secret Church is a lifestyle.*

Secret Church Versus Default Church

American Christians seem to have a built-in "default" button. Press it and the average American Christian will show up at a building on Sunday morning at 11 AM looking for a bulletin and a program, ready

> *American Christians seem to have a built-in "default" button.*

Secret Church

to sit for an hour-or-so while "others" (paid professional staff) "do" Church. That isn't church, not in the biblical sense. As A.W. Tozer described it a generation ago, and little has changed since.

"When we compare our present carefully programmed meetings with the New Testament we are reminded of the remark of a famous literary critic after he had read Alexander Pope's translation of Homer's Odyssey: 'It is a beautiful poem, but it is not Homer.' So the fast-paced, highly spiced, entertaining service of today may be a beautiful example of masterful programming - but it is not a Christian service. The two are leagues apart in almost every essential. About the only thing they have in common is the presence of a number of persons in one room. There the similarity ends and glaring dissimilarities begin." [45]

Secret Church doesn't have a default button. If it did, when pushed, the result would be a potluck in someone's home, worship together, ministry to each other based upon individual spiritual gifts and needs, and maybe even a discipleship study. The focus would be on building community, worshiping together, making disciples and finding ways to sow the seed of the Kingdom by serving those in need. Making the mental transition to Secret Church will take both time and intentional effort. And we may quickly discover that we have less time than we think. The urgency to move

---

[45] A.W. Tozer, **The Root Of The Righteous** (Camp Hill, PA: Wing Spread Publishers, 1955, 1986), page 105-106.

Secret Church

forward may well be determined by events which are beyond our control.

In order to help you reset your "default" button to organic Secret Church, allow me to offer you several resources which we have developed over the years, based upon our own experience. I want to break these resources into four basic areas.

1. Resources For Resetting Your Default Button To Secret Church - Resetting your "default" button to Secret Church takes time and effort. Trust me, I know. I've taken many of the lessons learned from our fifteen years of experience doing organic house church (in places ranging from private homes to homeless shelters) and put them into two books, ***River Houses Rising*** and ***Safe Houses Of Hope And Prayer***. [46] These two books will give you 33 chapters of challenging ideas covering a wide range of practical issues to help you re-set your "default" button for what it means to "be" the Church.

For example, in ***River Houses Rising*** you'll hear the story of *"the prophetic rain storm that didn't happen"* and what it means for the future of Secret Church. You'll discover more about the "Holy Discontent" that is moving more and more people into organic Secret Church; what it means to pursue a "Jesus-Shaped Spirituality"; how God uses the "Person of

---

[46] All of these resources are available via our website at risingrivermedia.org.

Secret Church

Peace" to sow the seed of the Kingdom, and the importance of Networking.

In *Safe Houses of Hope And Prayer*, the chapter entitled *"Honey, I Shrunk The Church"* is worth the price of the book all by itself. In Chapter 8 I tell *"The Parable Of The Shipwreck"* to illustrate the role of spiritual gifts in providing leadership in Secret Church. There are two chapters on the issue of money and the role of "radical sacrificial giving" as opposed to "tithing." My favorite chapter, on "Biblical Community," looks at building community using the 30+ "one anothers" found in the New Testament, but from the perspective of *"The Greatest Star Trek Episode Ever Made."* Trust me, you won't want to miss it!

2. Resources For Making Disciples Of The Kingdom - The Church of Jesus grows not by evangelism or by church planting, but by making disciples. The making of "disciples of the Kingdom" is God's plan for taking the good news of the Kingdom of God to the ends of the earth and for building His Church. We could honestly say that if you aren't making disciples (the way Jesus and the early Church made disciples), you really aren't participating in what God is doing.

Many (if not most) Christians never reproduce their faith by making disciples. Why? When we strip away all of the excuses, the answer is really quite simple: They don't know

> *Many (if not most) Christians never reproduce their faith by making disciples.*

Secret Church

how. They've never been given a model to follow (and a fill-in-the-blank workbook is NOT a model). They themselves were never really discipled by someone else. They don't know how, or where to start or what to do. That's why I wrote ***And They Dreamt Of A Kingdom: Biblical Studies In Discipleship And The Kingdom Of God*** (Volume 1 is currently available, and two additional volumes are under production.) I wrote this book (and the two to follow) to teach aspiring disciples and organic Church leaders to make disciples the way Jesus did by teaching them the same lessons Jesus taught His disciples. These books provide you with a tool to accomplish two key goals: 1) to help you better understand what it means to be "a disciple of the Kingdom," and 2) to provide you with what you need to disciple someone else (either individually, or in a group setting). Secret Church is about discipleship, not attendance.

3. Resources For Sowing The Kingdom By Serving Others - The importance of Christians manifesting the power of the Kingdom of God by serving those in need (people whom Jesus referred to as "the least of these" in Matthew 25:40&45) cannot be over stated. Author Richard Stearns calls it the hole in our gospel. It is so important that I have written two books on the subject. The first is entitled ***The Least of These: The Role of Good Deeds In A Jesus-Shaped Spirituality***. This book is the product of our own personal experiences of working among the homeless and marginalized over a ten-year period, and will answer many of your questions. The second book is entitled ***30 Days And 30 Ways Of Doing Good: Your Daily Guide To Greater***

Secret Church

Kindness And Good Deeds. This is a daily devotional and action guide designed to introduce you to a wide variety of issues, along with a daily devotional thought and suggested opportunities to get personally involved.

4. Resources For Pursuing Revival And Spiritual Awakening - During several years of fasting and praying for revival and spiritual awakening, God impressed me to write two books on the subject. The first is entitled, ***When Jesus Visits His Church.*** It is a study of Jesus' messages to the seven Churches of Asia in Revelation Chapters 2 and 3. When Jesus visits His people during times of spiritual revival, it is a visitation which brings both blessing and judgment. Jesus blesses our faithful obedience and judges our sin and disobedience (this isn't the "final" or "eternal" judgment, but the kind of judgment that produces conviction, confession and repentance over sin on a wide scale). His letters to the seven Churches reveal what pleases (and displeases) Him most, and it is an eye-opening study. Our second book on revival is entitled ***The Inextinguishable Blaze***. Every spiritual awakening is characterized by certain unique emphases which embody God's response to the spiritual condition of His people. Over the past several years of fasting and praying for revival, I have felt strongly impressed that, in the coming revival, God's emphasis is going to be upon restoring three things to His Church: 1) Holiness and the fear of the Lord, 2) Genuine personal repentance, and 3) Genuine personal intimacy with Him. This book is the story of those three things and God's pursuit to re-ignite *"The Inextinguishable Blaze"* in the hearts and lives of His people.

Secret Church

The Urgency Of The Hour

"We must work the works of him who sent me while it is day; night is coming, when no one can work." (John 9:4)

There is an urgency in the work of the Kingdom. There is an urgency to Secret Church. We began our journey into Secret Church with a proposition appropriate to our times, namely, that the moral and spiritual lights of the Kingdom are being systematically and intentionally switched off in America and the West. The result is the approach of a moral and spiritual Abyss of historic, even biblical proportions. The Church or our day must choose, either to join our collapsing civilization in its headlong plunge into the approaching Abyss, or to chart a different course. We call that different course organic Secret Church.

Welcome to Secret Church. Now, let's get busy.

Secret Church

Chapter 7
Underground Church

"And everyone kept feeling a sense of awe; and many wonders and signs were taking place through the apostles. And all those who had believed were together, and had all things in common; and they began selling their property and possessions, and were sharing them with all, as anyone might have need. And day by day continuing with one mind in the temple, and breaking bread from house to house, they were taking their meals together with gladness and sincerity of heart, praising God, and having favor with all the people. And the Lord was adding to their number day by day those who were being saved"(Acts 2:43-47).

Where Are The Lifeboats?

Perhaps you saw the 1997 blockbuster movie, "Titanic," the story of the ill-fated luxury liner "Titanic" which struck an ice berg on its maiden voyage on April 15, 1912, sinking and killing over 1,000 people. Early in the movie there is a scene in which the builder of the boat, Mr Andrews, (who perished in the disaster), explains to one of the lead characters that there are not sufficient lifeboats to accommodate all of the passengers. When asked why, the response is two-fold. First, the ship is unsinkable. Second, to install an additional row of lifeboats would crowd the decks and inconvenience the passengers.

> *Secret Church is about being a lifeboat.*

Secret Church

Secret Church is about being a lifeboat.

Too many Christians are building their lives and ministries on the assumption that America and the American Church are unsinkable. As we begin to prepare ourselves for the unfolding collapse of our culture and its plunge into the Abyss, our situation is not unlike that of the Titanic. The world system of this present darkness in which we live is similar to the Titanic. It is doomed and sinking. But most of the passengers are clueless. Having been assured by "competent authorities" that "not even God" could sink this ship they sail on, enjoying the benefits and ignoring the warnings. They will not believe that there is any danger until the ship is down 15 degrees and taking water over the bow. Only then (and some not even then) will they take note of their desperate situation and start looking for a lifeboat, if any are to be found.

> *Secret Church is about building lifeboats.*

Secret Church is about building lifeboats.

Difficult times, such as we have described in this book, are times when people go in search of a lifeboat. Seasons of revival and spiritual awakening are also such times when, in the Providence of God, the eyes of multitudes are opened to the reality of a "sinking" world system on the one hand, and the realities of the Kingdom of God on the other. The question today is whether or not the Church is prepared with

Underground Church

sufficient lifeboats to accommodate all those who will want to leave. According to Christian sociologist and trend-watcher George Barna, the answer is "no." Barna argues that the Church today is completely unprepared to handle the anticipated fruit of revival. Where are the classes and small groups needed to absorb, encourage and equip these new converts? According to reliable research a majority of the people who make a decision for Christ in one of our evangelical churches are not to be found in any church context within eight weeks of making that decision.[47] Our current church infrastructure is not adequate to retain and disciple the results of "normal" activity, much less the overwhelming stress that comes during times of revival, or from times of crisis, upheaval and collapse. In other words, we simply are not prepared for the consequences of the Abyss which now lies before us. The Titanic is sinking; there aren't enough lifeboats; the crew is debating whether or not to install a bistro; the passengers are clueless . . . and the worship band plays on.

Welcome to the new underground Church we are calling Secret Church. Underground Secret Church offers a structure which can absorb, encourage and disciple the fruit of revival while providing for the needs of people during difficult times (including persecution). Secret Church is

---

[47] This observation has been confirmed as accurate by a recent study conducted by the American Home Missions Board of the Southern Baptist Association which showed that of every 10 people who professed faith in Christ in a Southern Baptist Church, only one of those ten was still actively involved in the Church after one year.

Secret Church

nothing less than an underground community of organic churches networking quietly together and forming God's new underground Church. I

> *The "new thing" God does is seldom built upon the "old thing" we have done.*

believe that the next great movement of God's Spirit in power and revival will manifest itself in and through such an underground network of Secret Churches. Many traditional institutional churches are looking to revival and spiritual awakening in the hope that God will renew failed programs or dying institutions. But history tells us that this seldom happens. God seldom "revives" institutions or structures. The "new thing" God does is seldom built upon the "old thing" we have done. As Jesus warned us, new wine tends to destroy old wineskins (institutions or structures). New wine calls for new wineskins, and I believe that networking underground Secret Churches will be the new wineskin of the next great outpouring of God's Spirit in revival, renewal and awakening. Underground Secret Churches will prove to be BOTH a lifeboat AND a new wineskin.

Who Do You Trust?

Who do you turn to when times get tough? How much do you trust them? Enough to trust them with your life? How about the lives of your family and loved ones? Difficult times are coming upon both the church and the world: moral/spiritual collapse, terrorism, war, persecution, economic collapse; just to name a few of the things we have touched on in this

Underground Church

book. What we have collectively labeled "the Abyss." But regardless of the reason for or nature of the crisis, difficult times raise the same basic questions: Are you prepared to meet them and to manifest the Kingdom of God in the midst of such times? Who can you trust to help you through difficult times? Is your network of reliable people secure (and are they prepared to help)? Church History is filled with examples of how important reliable networks are during difficult times, but I want us to look briefly at three examples.

Early Christian Networks

What they were doing was illegal. What they were doing was believing. And that was dangerous. All Romans were "religious." They had a pantheon of gods and everyone was free to believe in any gods they chose, so long as they were also willing to acknowledge the "genius" of the divine Emperor by offering a pinch of incense upon altars dedicated to him. Romans would offer their pinch of incense with the usual incantation, "Caesar is Lord." By doing this, average Romans acknowledged the supremacy of the state in all practical matters.

But this new sect and its followers were different. They worshiped a god named "Chrestus" [48] or "Christ," a Jewish rabbi who had been crucified under Pontius Pilate in Palestine, but whom these people claimed had been raised

---

[48] Seutonius, *Life of Claudius*, 25.4. See also his *Lives of the Caesars*, 26.2.

Secret Church

from the dead. They rejected idols of all the gods (which had caused no small riot in the city of Ephesus), and refused to make any idol of their own god (which in Roman eyes was highly peculiar). In fact, they claimed that there was only one true God. It was rumored that they practiced cannibalism in their secret meetings (something about eating the body and drinking the blood of someone). But worst of all, they refused to acknowledge the "genius of the divine Emperor." They refused to acknowledge the "spirit of Rome" and the supremacy of the State. And this made them a threat.

For this reason, two of their leaders, one a former fisherman named Simon Peter and the other an itinerant Jewish philosopher named Saul (or Paul) of Tarsus, had been arrested, tried for sedition and treason against the Emperor, and had been executed as enemies against the State. This had taken place under Emperor Nero, around A.D. 65. From that time onward, for the next 250 years (until Emperor Constantine) it was a criminal offense against the State, punishable by death, to openly profess Christianity. Although actual persecutions were sporadic and localized (but intense when they occurred), the threat was real and constant. The mere accusation by a neighbor, friend or acquaintance could mean arrest, imprisonment, a challenge to confess or renounce, and death.

> *They refused to acknowledge the "spirit of Rome" and the supremacy of the State. And this made them a threat.*

Underground Church

In order to pursue their faith without drawing attention to themselves these early Christians were forced to take unusual steps. The early Church was forced to become an underground networking church. They became a "Secret Church." As the above passage from the Book of Acts demonstrates, the early Church had always been a networking church (The Book of Acts was written, prior to the beginning of official Roman persecutions). The anonymous author of the New Testament book of Hebrews admonished believers, *"let us consider how to stimulate one another to love and good deeds, not forsaking our own assembling together, as is the habit of some, but encouraging one another; and all the more, as you see the day drawing near"* (Hebrews 10:24-25). This was simple first century networking among Christian believers. They met in homes and ministered to one another privately, while also attending public worship at the Temple and in local synagogues. People associated with the early Church openly and the Church freely accepted all who came.

But once the official Roman persecutions began, certain things had to change. Churches began to meet secretly in members' homes, or in secret locations (such as in the subterranean catacombs beneath the city of Rome). In order to identify themselves to fellow believers (or to prevent identifying themselves to hostile non-believers) they created "secret signs" including the sign of the fish. In Greek, the word "fish" ($IX\Theta Y\Sigma$ or *ichthus*) represented an "acrostic" where each letter represented the first word in the following phrase in Greek: Jesus (I) Christ © God's (Θ) Son (Υ)

Secret Church

Saviour (Σ). By drawing the sign of a fish one believer could identify himself as a Christian to a fellow believer (who would acknowledge the sign), but a non-believer would ignore the cryptic message. In difficult times you need to be able to identify and network with people whom you know you can trust.

The Underground Railroad Network

What they were doing was illegal. Some of them were escaping slavery for freedom. Others were helping them to escape. Both groups were breaking the law. In 1831 a runaway slave named Tice Davids fled from Kentucky

> *Some of them were escaping slavery for freedom. Others were helping them to escape. Both groups were breaking the law.*

and took refuge with one John Rankin, a white abolitionist in Ripley, Ohio. Determined to retrieve his "escaped property," the owner chased Davids as far as the Ohio River. But Davids suddenly disappeared without a trace, leaving his bewildered owner wondering if the slave had *"gone off on some underground railroad."*

For the next 30 years the "underground railroad" would assist thousands of escaped slaves to find freedom in the northern U.S. and Canada. Not even the passage in 1850 of a revised "Fugitive Slave Law," which required federal and state officials as well as private citizens to assist in the capture and return of escaped slaves, would stop the railroad from

Underground Church

operating. Escaped slaves became "passengers." People assisting in their escape were "agents." Those escorting the "passengers" were called "conductors." Back roads, rivers and trails were "rails." And the safe houses along the way providing food, shelter and money were "stations." Station "operators" would notify runaways of the station's existence with simple signals such as a brightly lit candle in the window or by a lantern strategically placed in the front yard. The stations provided safety and rest in concealed rooms, attics and cellars. It was a secret network that operated during difficult times. Even today, not much is known about how the Underground Railroad operated because "agents" usually hid or destroyed their personal journals and records in order to protect themselves and their "passengers." This network saved thousands of lives over the 25 years that it operated.

The Hiding Place Network

What they were doing was illegal. What they were doing was giving refuge and asylum to political refugees. Theirs was a devout Dutch Reformed family. For several generations their family had owned and operated a watch shop in the lower level of the family home in the little town of Haarlem in the Netherlands. Their business contacts with Jewish businessmen in Germany had alerted them to the growing threat of Nazism. But what could they do? The eldest son, Wilhelm, had

> *What they were doing was illegal. What they were doing was giving refuge and asylum to political refugees.*

Secret Church

studied for the ministry. He now joined the growing Dutch underground, helping to sabotage German war installations and providing escape routes for Jews fleeing persecution. Word spread among Jewish refugees that the old watchmaker, Herr ten Boom, and his two daughters, Corrie and Betsy, could be trusted. The hidden passages and attic nooks of their three-story house became a sanctuary for Jewish refugees (who were referred to in code as "clocks" and "watches"). But in 1944 their home and watch shop was raided by the Gestapo. They had been betrayed, but not by a German spy. Corrie ten Boom would spend the next year in a Nazis concentration camp (Corrie's father and her sister Betsy would die there), because they had been betrayed by a fellow Dutchman (and probably a fellow "church-goer") who had suspected them of being "Jewish sympathizers."

The Importance of Networks

As the above historical examples illustrate, in times of collapse and crisis, it is critical to know who you can trust. That's the role of a community and a network. The importance of networks was summed up by Christian philosopher C. S. Lewis when he described the significance of close friendships. Listen to what he said:

"Every friendship is a sort of secession, even a rebellion. It may be a rebellion of serious thinkers against accepted claptrap or of faddists against accepted good sense; of real artists against popular ugliness or of charlatans against civilized taste; of good men against the badness of society or

Underground Church

of bad men against its goodness. Whatever it is, it will be unwelcome to Top People. In each knot of friends, there is a section which fortifies its members against the public opinion of the community in general. Each is therefore a pocket of potential resistance. Men who have real friends are less easy to manage or "get at;" harder for bad authorities to corrupt. Hence, if our masters, by force or by propaganda about "togetherness" or by unobtrusively making privacy impossible, ever succeed in producing a world in which all are companions and none are friends, they will have removed certain dangers, and will also have taken from us what is almost our strongest safeguard against complete servitude." C. S. Lewis, ***The Four Loves***)

At it's very core, a network of underground Secret Churches represents a gathering of friends and believers, who have come together to "be" the Church, and to meet one another's needs in a bond of trust and mutual commitment. So once again we are confronted with the question, *"Who do you trust?"* Who are those individuals whom you call "friends." Not only does history demonstrate the need for networks of like-minded people who work together to support and encourage one another during difficult times, but Scripture positively commands it. I believe this is what the writer of Hebrews means in Chapter 10 where he says:

"Let us hold fast the confession of our hope without wavering, for he who promised is faithful. And let us consider how to stir up one another to love and good works, not neglecting to meet together, as is the habit of some, but

Secret Church

encouraging one another, and all the more as you see the Day drawing near." (Hebrews 10:23-25)

I believe the writer clearly lays out the three-fold purpose of gathering together as a community of Secret Churches. The **first purpose** we gather together for is to encourage each other to "hold fast" the confession of our hope and faith in Jesus and the Kingdom. This was a "big deal" in the early underground Church, particularly as persecution increased and believers experienced intense pressure to compromise their faith with the surrounding culture. In the letters to the seven churches of Asia, the Risen Christ commends the persecuted Christians in Pergamum for holding fast and not denying His Name (Revelation 2:13) in the face of intense persecution. He also admonishes the believers in Thyatira (Rev. 2:25) and Philadelphia (Rev. 3:11) to do the same and to *"hold fast what you have."* [49] What does "holding fast" look like in your life? Where are you being challenged by the collapsing world system to compromise your faith and your obedience? As our culture collapses and plunges into the moral and spiritual Abyss, increased pressure will be brought to bear upon Christians to compromise in a wider variety of areas.

The **second purpose** we gather together for in Secret Church is to *"stir up one another to love and good deeds."*

---

[49] You'll find more on the issue of holding fast versus compromise in our book, ***When Jesus Visits His Church: Studies in The Seven Churches of Asia (Revelation 2-3)***, available via our website at risingrivermedia.org.

Underground Church

The English rendering of "stir up" doesn't quite do justice to the Greek word *paroxumos*, which communicates the idea of "inciting" or "provoking" someone to the point of sharp disagreement. One of the purposes of assembling together as believers in Secret Church is so that we can give careful thought and study as to how we can incite and provoke one another to good deeds. This is important. In *"Chapter 11 - Becoming Legendary For Our Good Deeds"* of **Safe Houses of Hope And Prayer** I talk about the importance of Secret Churches engaging in good deeds. Like those early Christians we discovered who became "legendary" for ministering to plague victims in ancient Rome, your Secret Church needs a plan for how you intend to obey Jesus' admonitions in Matthew 25:34-46 and to "become legendary" for your good deeds.

The **third purpose** we gather together for in Secret Church is to encourage one another in light of the Lord's soon return. This passage is particularly relevant to believers today. The day the writer refers to as "drawing near" is the day of Christ's return. If we truly believe that we are approaching the End of the Age and that the day of Christ's return is drawing near, then the writer of Hebrews warns us that it is particularly important that we not forsake the assembling of ourselves for mutual support and encouragement. Let's be clear. As our culture's headlong plunge into the Abyss accelerates, things are going to get dark. Difficult times lie ahead for the Church. The purpose of Secret Church is to encourage one another to "hold fast" during these challenging times, while reminding each other of God's

Secret Church

faithfulness toward His people in difficult times. It is important that we be networking together in Secret Church.

As this plunge into the Abyss unfolds, our challenge will be that crises move at the speed of computers, emails, texts, Twitter and Facebook. We may have little (if any) warning that a crisis is impending. As I said in the Introduction to this book, one morning, in the near future, you will wake up, turn on the morning news and discover that the world you once knew is gone. By the time a crisis is upon us it will be too late to begin building a reliable support network. Networks are composed of relationships, and like good relationships, good networks take time to build.

Back To The Future

As Christians now living in a Post-Christian, Postmodern culture that is increasingly and openly hostile towards Christianity, it is time for us to recognize and embrace the reality of our situation: we are an underground Church and a counter-cultural witness to a formerly Christian culture, now in the fading twilight of its former greatness. What little light remains is not the dawn of a new age, but the light thrown off by fading embers of what once burned brightly. In its spiritual blindness, our Postmodern culture mistakes the darkness of the approaching Abyss for light.

As our culture's headlong plunge into the Abyss unfolds, the contemporary Church will discover that it has many things in common with the Church of the 1st Century, including the

Underground Church

reality of being a counter-cultural witness to an increasingly pagan culture in the late stages of decline and collapse.

It didn't take long for the early Christian Church to find itself in the position of being a counter-cultural witness on two fronts. For the first 35 years of its existence the Church was a counter-cultural witness to an institutional Judaism which had rejected Jesus as the Messiah and which actively engaged in sporadic persecutions of "the Way." We see this both in the Book of Acts, and in the letters of the Risen Christ to the seven Churches of Asia in Revelation Chapters 2-3.[50] Official Judaism's persecution of the Church continued until the destruction of Jerusalem and the Temple put an end to institutional Judaism itself in A.D. 70. But around A.D. 64 Christianity also found itself forced into the position of being a counter-cultural witness to the dominant Roman culture. Following the fiery conflagration that consumed a good part of the city of Rome in July of A.D. 64, the Emperor Nero blamed the disaster upon the Christians and declared the profession of Christian faith to be a capital offense, punishable by death. For the next 250 years Christianity existed as an underground network of organic house churches, and Christians lived their lives as a counter-cultural witness to a secular culture in decline. It is probably safe to say that nearly every New Testament Epistle

---

[50] This hostility between Judaism and the Church is seen in the phrase *"synagogue of Satan"* in Revelation 2:9 ad 3:9. See our book, ***When Jesus Visits His Church: Studies in The Seven Churches of Asia (Revelation 2-3)***, available via our website at risingrivermedia.org.

Secret Church

was written to an organic house church, or to an individual who had a Secret Church meeting in his house. For the first 250 years of its existence, Christianity consisted of groups of believers who met secretly for worship in private homes. Author and New Testament scholar Bradley Blue, in an article entitled *"Acts And The House Church,"* summarizes this period as follows:

"Recent archaeological evidence from such diverse places as Capernaum, Rome and Kent strongly suggests that for the first few hundred years of the Church's existence, Christian groups gathered, not in large 'purpose-built' church buildings, but in domestic residences which could accommodate their needs. Sometimes these were renovated better to fit the needs of the community, but in at least one case (Dura-Europos) the internal renovations were carefully made invisible externally. The book of Acts mentions such figures as Aquila and Priscilla, Jason of Thessalonica, Simon the Tanner, Lydia and the Philippian Jailor (and their homes and hospitality) not merely out of gratitude for offering Christian leaders a place to sleep, but probably because they opened their homes for meetings of their local Christian communities." [51]

This period of official persecution of Christians, from the reign of Nero in A.D. 64 until the Emperor Constantine and

---

[51] Bradley Blue, *"Acts And The House Church,"* in ***The Book of Acts In Its First Century Setting***, Volume 2, David W. J. Gill and Conrad Gempf, eds. (Grand Rapids: William B. Eerdmans Publishing Company, 1994), p. 119 - 222.

Underground Church

the Edict of Nantes in A.D. 313, prevented Christians from building dedicated buildings for Christian gatherings. Structures were limited to private residences which were occasionally renovated to accommodate large groups of Christian worshipers. But even this was risky since such residences could be identified, seized and even destroyed.

The ascension of Constantine to the Imperial Throne of Rome and the cessation of official persecution resulted in a building spree, encouraged by Constantine himself, who ordered Christian property restored and ordered the building of numerous "basilicas" or dedicated places of Christian worship throughout the Empire. Christians, having endured the prior 50 years of "The Great Persecution," began to congregate publicly in dedicated public buildings (called "basilicas")for the first time in nearly 250 years.

Deja vu All Over Again?

Historians estimate that, when Christianity finally triumphed over Rome in the Fourth Century, Christians constituted around 5% of the population of the Empire. In an Empire of roughly 60 million people this meant roughly 3 million Christians. In other words, the faith of that early church was so virulent that their impact upon Roman society was completely

> *. . . the faith of that early church was so virulent that their impact upon Roman society was completely out of proportion to their numbers.*

Secret Church

out of proportion to their numbers, and their influence upon their society was growing, not fading. Today, 17 centuries later, the situation is reversed. Roughly 80% of all American adults self-identify as "Christian" and approximately 25% of Americans profess to be "born again Christians." Yet, Christianity is quickly becoming a counter cultural movement whose influence is fading. Once again, Christians are having an effect that is disproportionate to their numbers, only in reverse. Perhaps this is why, in the Providence of God, He is once again calling His people "back to basics," back to being an underground, networking Secret Church, re-establishing a virulent counter-cultural faith and witness, raising up a "new" wineskin which is actually 2,000 years old. Welcome to Secret Church.

Characteristics of Underground Secret Church

As we have seen, the concept of an underground Secret Church is not new. It is where Christianity started, going all the way back to the Book of Acts. But there is always a timing in God's work among His people. That timing reveals God's Kingdom purposes. One of the most recent examples of God's timing in raising up underground Secret Churches is in China. The growth of underground Secret Churches (primarily, organic house churches) in China came about as the result of intense and on-going persecution by the Chinese communists during the dark days of the Cultural Revolution (1966-1978). The Chinese underground house church movement exploded in secret, surprising most Western Church "experts" who feared that the Chinese

Underground Church

Church would not survive the expulsion of western missionaries (in 1952) or the dissolution of the denominations (in 1958) or the terrible persecution of Christians which followed during the 1960s and 70s. So, what are some of the characteristics of secret, underground, networking, organic house churches which make them so effective and attractive?[52] Consider the following:

1. Simplicity - There is a reason why organic house church is often referred to as "simple church." It really is both simple and flexible in design. The complicated, high-input-low-output, resource intensive, high-overhead model of church is all but eliminated. There is little or no "hierarchy." Families and friends meet together for fellowship, worship, prayer, mutual ministry, the meeting of each other's needs and the serving of others in need.

2. Gifted/Anointed Leadership - Secret Church is led by individuals based upon the gifts God has given to each person within the group. The believing community recognizes and acknowledges people, their unique gifts and the anointing of the Holy Spirit. The issue isn't seminary education or denominational appointment, but whom has the Holy Spirit gifted and anointed (see Chapters 7 and 8 of my book *Safe Houses of Hope And Prayer*, available via our website at risingrivermedia.org).

---

[52] These characteristics are discussed by Arthur Wallis, *China Miracle: A Silent Explosion*, Cityhill Publishing, 4600 Christian Fellowship Road, Columbia, Mo. 65203 ISBN-13: 978-0939159000

Secret Church

3. Group Participation - The best description of an organic church gathering is that *"everyone participates, but no one dominates."* Organic Secret Church allows for each person to exercise his or her God-given spiritual gift, just as Paul instructs in 1 Corinthians 14:26.

4. End-time Flexibility - The organic house church structure of Secret Church is uniquely designed to accommodate the "end-time shaking" predicted by Scripture (see Hebrews 12:25-29). It can meet anywhere (in a home, a coffee shop, a business, a restaurant, a barn, on a roof-top, and anywhere else people can gather) and respond quickly to changing conditions.

5. Persecution Resistant Structure - Its low-profile and flexibility make the networking Secret Church difficult to find and even more difficult to persecute. As Arthur Wallis notes, *"The more imposing the edifice, the more easily it is found by the gunner. The more obvious and obtrusive an organization, the more ready it is attacked and ruined."* [53] Persecuting a networking community of believers who can meet house-to-house or place-to-place is like trying to nail Jello to a tree!

6. Easy Multiplication - The organic house church structure of Secret Church is uniquely designed to accommodate quick and easy multiplication and duplication. As groups grow in size and leaders arise, groups split off to form new groups meeting in new homes, but remaining in fellowship

---

[53] Wallis, ***China Miracle***, page 150.

Underground Church

and community with the group they came from, so that a network is born and grows (See our discussion on the power of multiplication versus addition in *"Chapter 13 - God Has A Math Problem"* of ***River Houses Rising***, available via our website).

7. Genuine "Lifestyle Evangelism" *-* Secret Churches offer a friendly and inclusive environment where the gospel can be shared one-on-one as part of a biblical lifestyle and where "disciples" replace "converts."

8. It Is Biblical *-* It should be abundantly clear at this point that Secret Church IS New Testament Church and New Testament Church IS Secret Church. It is not possible to understand the Church of the New Testament without understanding that the New Testament was written to believers in a network of underground Secret Churches meeting house-to-house.

Where To Begin

We have already seen that Secret Church isn't a program. It's a lifestyle. And as part of our lifestyle, we already have a loose network of friends and family that we rely on when times get tough. Now we need to become more intentional about expanding and strengthening our networks. It is sad but true that the average multi-level marketer is more organized, excited and committed to building a sales network to sell his or her "can't-live-without" widget than the average Christian is about building a community of people committed

Secret Church

to sharing the gospel and expanding the Kingdom of God!

Make A List. Begin making a prayer list of people to pray for and to challenge concerning Secret Church. The idea here is quite simple. Begin with people within your own circle of influence, people with whom you already share some common Christian interests. I have been amazed and pleasantly surprised to discover many fellow believers who have silently shared my concerns.

Pray! Begin praying regularly for each of the names on your list. Pray that God would prepare and challenge their hearts, making them receptive to what He is doing in our day.

Give. Give each person on your list a copy of this book. If they aren't interested, or if they aren't willing to read and educate themselves, or if they respond negatively, then you know that either the timing is wrong and they aren't ready, or that they simply aren't the kind of people who could be successful participants in a Secret Church community.

Invite. Now it's time for a potluck. Invite those people who took a book, and who responded with interest, to a potluck (yep, everyone bring something to share). Have a time of discussion, sharing and prayer. Discuss the book as a starting point to share your mutual interests and concerns. The starting point of any successful network is to "educate and motivate" people, because people need a reason to get out of their comfort zones. Discussing the book and the issues it raises is a good way to accomplish this.

Underground Church

Commit. As people respond to discussions regarding Secret Church, invite them to begin meeting regularly. Maybe it begins with a monthly gathering for food (yep, another potluck!) for fellowship, discussion, prayer, encouragement, study of the word, and ministry. Before you know it, your Secret Church will be under way! Eventually, as your group continues to grow and mature, you'll challenge each member of your Secret Church to repeat this process, each person making their own list, challenging people to join the group which will eventually split off to form separate Secret Church groups. Members of your group may, in fact, be leading or participating in one or more other networking Secret Church groups. That's how a networking community grows and reproduces (I devote 2 Chapters [15 and 16] to networking in my book *River Houses Rising*).

Educate Yourself. It's important to become a student of your craft, even the "craft" of Secret Church. In the previous Chapter (6) I gave a number of organic church resources. In addition to those organic church oriented resources, I would also encourage you to read the histories of other networks to learn how they have historically operated during times of emergency, crisis or war. I have personally benefitted by reading histories of World War 2 underground resistance movements and their networks.[54]

---

[54] A good overall treatment of World War 2 European resistance movements is D. A. Lande, *Resistance!: Occupied Europe And Its Defiance Of Hitler* (Osceola, WI: MBI Publsihing Company, 2000). See also Arthur Wallis, *China Miracle: A Silent Explosion* (Columbia, MO: Cityhill Publishing)

Secret Church

More Ideas For Building Your Secret Church Network

Secret Church will be a challenge for many believers for the simple reason that it isn't a step-by-step program, but a lifestyle. And because Secret Church is a lifestyle instead of a program, it is impossible to give a simple formula for how to go about building a network of believers committed to a common cause.[55] Networks are made up of people, which means that, in its essence, a network is a system of inter-connected relationships. People are not perfect, and both their strengths and their imperfections will manifest themselves in your network. Remember *"Maurice's Maxim # 1: Life Is Messy!"* Secret Church networks, like all relationships, require the willingness and the ability of leaders and participants to acknowledge and forgive one another's imperfections, and to exercise love and forbearance toward one another (see Ephesians 4:32).

What follows are some principles to use in evaluating people, and in overseeing your network. Not all of them will apply(again, this is not a formula). They are intended to stimulate your thinking as you seek to make wise decisions

---

[55] One of the classic books on this topic of organizing and motivating networks is by Douglas Hyde, entitled ***Dedication and Leadership*** (Notre Dame: University of Notre Dame Press, 1966). Hyde was a communist for 20 years and news editor of the *London Daily Worker*. He became disillusioned with communism and was converted to Christianity. In this book he reflects on the principles and strategies used by communist leadership to recruit, train and motivate people in their networks. Another good resource is Elton Trueblood, ***The Company of the Committed*** (San Francisco: Harper & Roe Publishers, 1961, 1980).

Underground Church

about inviting people into the "inner circle" of your important Secret Church contacts. Remember: you are not seeking to find other "perfect people," but you are attempting to find other fellow believers who understand the challenging times which lie ahead, and who share your values, your concerns and your desire to be a "disciple of the Kingdom" in our Post-Christian Postmodern culture.

1. Do you know them well, or do they come on the recommendation of someone you know well? You will one day be trusting them for your safety, your welfare and perhaps your life.

2. Do they demonstrate a hunger for God which manifests itself in such characteristics as a teachable spirit, a practical knowledge of Scripture, a worshipful heart towards God and a consistent life of prayer.

3. Do they demonstrate a servant's heart towards others, willing to make personal sacrifices in order to serve others? Do they demonstrate gifts or abilities of leadership or of service?

4. Do they demonstrate the ability to exercise discretion and to keep confident those things shared with them in confidence? Remember the old World War 2 proverb: "Loose lips sink ships"!

5. Does their "talk" match their "walk." If not, think twice. Then think again.

Secret Church

6. Do they have skills, hobbies or interests that you and those in your network need or need to learn (carpentry, electrical, small engine repair, locksmith, ham radio operator, etc.).

7. Do they appear to exercise good common sense in practical matters and decision making?

8. Do they "walk with a limp?" Like Jacob who wrestled with God in the wilderness(Genesis 32:24-32), I am referring to believers who have wrestled with God and with the problems of life. They have won their personal battles and have prevailed with God, but they walk with a limp as a sign of the struggle. These are believers who understand the messiness of life because they have experienced it for themselves, have learned to deal with it at the Throne of Grace, and who have sacrificed their pride and judgmentalism for compassion and grace.

9. Do they worship "idols"? Idols come in many forms. Some people worship idols of materialism and financial success and are unable to see the Church as anything other than a gathering of affluent upper-middle-class Americans. Some worship idols of church structure, denominations, or theology and are unable to subordinate these things to the Kingdom of God. Others worship idols of particular social issues (conservative politics, abortion, pornography, etc). It is critical that each of us identify

Underground Church

our personal "idols" and deal with them.

10. Are they willing to live in peace and community with other members of the Secret Church network?

People To Avoid

1. Avoid Contentious People. Avoid allowing into your community people who demonstrate an argumentative or contentious spirit, wanting to argue over small points of doctrine, or push a particular church, denomination, or doctrine. A contentious or argumentative spirit is a divisive spirit. The goal here is not to judge people, or to squelch discussion. The goal is to promote the peace of the Church and to avoid people who will disrupt that peace with a contentious (and usually unteachable) spirit.

2. Avoid Agendized People. Avoid people who are seeking to push particular theological-political-social agendas. As someone who founded a pro-life advocacy group, has staged anti-abortion rallies, founded a prepared food rescue agency to feed those in need, and served as a director of a men's homeless shelter, I understand issues, passion and agendas. I am not saying that Christians and Secret Churches should not be involved in such activities. I believe Christians and Secret Churches should be politically and socially active as an expression of Kingdom values and as a witness to our Post-Christian Postmodern Culture. But beware of individuals who want to join groups in order to recruit members to their particular cause or agenda. Remember, God's primary

Secret Church

agenda, which comes before all others, is to build up His Church and to expand His Kingdom in the hearts, homes and lives of His people. God's agenda has always been - and continues to be - discipleship and the Kingdom of God. This is the well-spring from which everything else flows!

3. Avoid Angry People. Avoid people who are motivated by anger, bitterness and resentment towards the government, or the organized church, etc. People who are motivated by such feelings are often contentious, divisive and are frequently out to "grind an axe" with someone, and they'll eventually end up grinding it on you. Good ministry never springs from the well of an angry, bitter heart (I would encourage you to read *"Chapter 4 - Honey, I Shrunk The Church"* of **Safe Houses of Hope And Prayer** where I talk about the importance of "detoxing").

4. Avoid False Teachers. Avoid people who want to be part of your Secret Church fellowship so they can find an audience for their "special teaching." False teachers are to the New Testament what false prophets were to the Old Testament; people to be avoided at all costs. The New Testament book of 2 John is helpful if you need biblical instruction on this issue (I deal more extensively with false teachers and false doctrine in *"Chapter 15 - Beware The Wanderers"* of **Safe Houses of Hope And Prayer**).

Underground Church

Secret Church Leadership

In my book, ***Safe Houses of Hope And Prayer***, I devote two chapters (Chapters 7 and 8) to the issue of leadership, which is more than I can do here. I would strongly encourage you to get a copy of that book. But I want to tell two quick stories concerning leadership in Secret Church. Several years ago, at an organic house church conference, I was privileged to attend a leadership workshop led by George Barna. In that workshop, Barna talked about the characteristics of revolutionary leaders. One in particular that caught my attention was this: Good leaders set people up for success in their absence. The role of a leader - any leader - in Secret Church is to set up those you lead for success in your absence. The more dependent you make people upon you, the less successful you will be as a leader. Why? Because you are setting them up for failure when you (or they) leave. Jesus spent over three years setting His disciples up to succeed in His absence. That's biblical leadership, and that is how we are to disciple others.

> *Good leaders set people up for success in their absence.*

My second story comes from one of my early mentors, Dr. Harold O. J. ("Joe") Brown. I was privileged to be Joe's teaching assistant for a summer course in "Cultural Apologetics." In one of his excellent lectures, he defined biblical "authority" as *"the ability to command voluntary obedience."* There are many "false leaders" in the Church

Secret Church

today, people claiming to exercise authority over others which, biblically speaking, they simply do NOT possess. They are false leaders exercising false authority, for which God will hold them accountable on the Day of Judgment.

In organic Secret Church, leadership functions on the basis of spiritual gifts, not position or office, and in Chapters 7 and 8 of *Safe Houses of Hope And Prayer* I identify the seven leadership gifts or callings which operate in the Church. In Secret Church (or ANY Church, for that matter) leaders exercise an authority which embodies the ability to *"command voluntary obedience"* among those they serve. This is NOT the authority to lord it over others. It is the authority which flows from the combination of a recognized spiritual gift and a Christ-like example of sacrificial service. Such a combination results in the ability to encourage those under their care, to facilitate discussion and interaction, to communicate reliable information, to be a problem solver, a reconciler of conflicts and a peace maker. In short, biblical leadership in Secret Church is about serving others, not ruling them.

Beginning Suggestions

O.K., let's get down to some practical "brass tacks" (as my momma used to say). Allow me to make a few suggestions.

Suggestion # 1. I would encourage you to consider limiting the size of your Secret Church to around 8 families (or 15-20 participants). Larger groups quickly become unwieldy and

Underground Church

difficult to manage effectively (not to mention that you need a large living room to accommodate that many people). Two Secret Church groups of 5 families are better than 1 Secret Church group of 10 families (although occasionally meeting together as one large group is a good idea, so everyone can get to know each other). Better to "multiply" than to simply "grow."

Suggestion # 2. At either your first or second meeting, I would encourage you to establish a regular meeting time for your group. It's important for everyone to treat the meeting time as a high priority, while being flexible and not becoming "legalistic." It is also a good idea to establish a habit of moving around from "house-to-house" (or "place-to-place") so that no one feels left out and people get to know each other in their natural home environment. Establish a regular meeting schedule and make certain that each member knows the time and location.

Suggestion # 3. Early in your first several meetings you should discuss where you want to go as a group. What will be your spiritual focus? A bible study? A devotional study? A discipleship study? I would encourage you to consider a focus on what it means to be a "disciple of the Kingdom" and how to make disciples. This is why I wrote my book on discipleship, ***And They Dreamt Of A Kingdom: Biblical Studies On Discipleship And The Kingdom Of God - Volume 1*** (two more Volumes are under production). Volume 1 contains 42 lessons on discipleship, built around how Jesus worked with His 12 disciples. There is literally a year's

Secret Church

worth of Secret Church lessons on discipleship in Volume 1 alone. I would encourage you to consider using it to set the tone of what your Secret Church is all about: making disciples who will be able to make disciples.

Suggestion # 4. Early on, have a serious discussion concerning how you as individuals and as a group intend to engage in outreach by serving *"the least of these."* The tone of making disciples (see above) must be matched with a tone of serving others, as Jesus expects in Matthew 25:31-46. Without an outward focus of outreach, your fellowship will become insular, isolated and inward . . . and ineffective. Your fellowship is like your faith, it is either growing or dying. No middle ground. I would encourage you to get our two books which I wrote to encourage believers in this area: **The Least of These** and **30 Days And 30 Ways of Doing Good**, both available via our website.

There is no magic formula for conducting a Secret Church gathering. Every gathering should be led by the Holy Spirit, and each particular Secret Church group must learn how to listen to the voice of the Holy Spirit for themselves, while at the same time pursuing a mutually agreed upon direction. Consider the following as a *possible* guide for a Secret Church gathering:

1. **Food!** Hold a potluck. People tend to relax over and around food. It is also a great time for people to get their personal "visiting" out of the way.

Underground Church

2. **Communion.** Toward the end of the meal, celebrate communion. I like to use Paul's words in 1 Corinthians 11:23-26:

   "For I received from the Lord what I also delivered to you, that the Lord Jesus on the night when he was betrayed took bread, and when he had given thanks, he broke it, and said, 'This is my body which is for you. Do this in remembrance of me.' In the same way also he took the cup, after supper, saying, 'This cup is the new covenant in my blood. Do this, as often as you drink it, in remembrance of me.' For as often as you eat this bread and drink the cup, you proclaim the Lord's death until he comes."

3. **Prayer And Worship.** Spend extended time in prayer and worship. Invite the Holy Spirit to guide you into His "agenda" for your time together.

4. **Spiritual Emphasis.** This is the time to focus your attention on the Lord and the Word. Use a guided Bible Study or book study as needed and agreed upon by the group.

5. **Personal Prayer and Ministry Time.** People have personal needs which they need to express and ask for prayer or counsel. People also have ministry gifts which they need to exercise in ministering to one another. One of the vital community building functions of Secret Church is sharing our lives in all their

Secret Church

messiness so that we come to love and appreciate one another, and to trust what God is doing in our midst. Do not neglect this time. You will discover over time that your Secret Church will regard this as one of the most important times of the entire meeting.

6. **Adjourn & Fellowship**. Over the years we have learned that meetings tend to "adjourn themselves" as prayer and ministry wind down. It is a good sign of a growing sense of community when people want to linger and visit and enjoy one another's company.

Remember: there is no magic formula (and no program!) for a successful Secret Church gathering.

Additional Secret Church resources are available on our website at *risingrivermedia.org*.

www.ingramcontent.com/pod-product-compliance
Lightning Source LLC
Chambersburg PA
CBHW070154100426
42743CB00013B/2906

9780996009676